Historic Portsmouth

HARD
HARTFORD FIRE INSURANCE CO
HENRY LEVEN

Historic Portsmouth

Early Photographs from the Collections of Strawbery Banke, Inc.

Text by James L. Garvin

New Hampshire Publishing Company
Somersworth
1974

Library of Congress Catalog Card Number: 73-76394
Standard Book Number: 0-912274-32-8
Printed in the United States of America

Front Cover:
Looking west on Congress Street, Portsmouth, during the early 1890s.

Frontispiece:
Portsmouth's Market Square during the 1880s, its trees bowed under the burden of a wet snow.

Back Cover:
The Wentworth Hotel in New Castle in 1886, with the steam ferry Gypsy *posing at the pier.*

Preface

Portsmouth, New Hampshire, is one of the oldest communities in the United States. Historically, it is also one of the richest, and has preserved an unusual number of its streets, buildings, and other landmarks essentially unchanged. Other colonial towns, once as lavishly endowed with historical remains, often exchanged their heritages for growth, modernization, and commercial prosperity. Portsmouth, paying the price of a relative quiescence during America's industrial age, preserved its special character.

This is not to say that time has not touched the old town by the sea. From the late nineteenth century down to the present day, an appalling number of Portsmouth's landmarks have been ruthlessly stripped, dismantled, or burned. Modernizations beginning before the turn of this century destroyed the ancient character of the great navy yard on Dennett's and Seavey's Islands. Urban renewal has seriously altered the face of Portsmouth's South End, and has virtually obliterated the North End. And, at a rate that has increased yearly since 1900, Portsmouth's fine old buildings have individually fallen to the wrecker's machinery or been carelessly denatured in the name of progress.

It is time, then, for these photographs to be published. It is time for those who know Portsmouth as it is today to see Portsmouth as it was yesterday; for those residents and visitors who are captivated by the town's individuality to see that this individuality springs from a strong and unique local character that was once far more pronounced than it is in the twentieth century. No one, whether native, newcomer, or visitor, can see these pictures without experiencing a sense of loss and a deep regret that more traces of Portsmouth's early culture have not been preserved. One can only ask whether the losses have been balanced by the gains as Portsmouth has evolved from a nineteenth-century town into a twentieth-century city.

Fortunately there are many persons today with a keen interest in Portsmouth's past. Many of these showed unbounded willingness to help with this book. These individuals bear no responsibility for the shortcomings of the following pages, but deserve much of the credit for any contributions the volume may make. I am especially indebted to Mrs. Garland W. Patch, Sr., who was extremely generous with her time and with the resources at her command. Mrs. Patch not only provided information on the acquisition of the priceless negative collection assembled by her late husband, but offered invaluable reminiscences and historical facts. Mrs. Perley N. Storer provided critical material on the early life of Caleb S. Gurney, who was Portsmouth's first photographer with a true historical perspective. Arthur J. Sherburne of Portsmouth, Mrs. Violet Sawyer of Mechanic Falls, Maine, and Mrs. Lawrence L. Davis of West Minot, Maine, were also of great help in offering information on Gurney. Alvah C. Card provided a wealth of helpful reminiscences. Raymond A. Brighton, author of *They Came to Fish*, performed a great service to everyone interested in photographic history by publishing an account of Samuel P. Long's first daguerrean experiments in 1840.

I am indebted to Edmund E. Lynch, Director of Strawbery Banke, and to the Strawbery Banke staff and trustees for permitting and encouraging me to relinquish my other duties while completing this book. And I owe sincere thanks to Frank Donegan for innumerable insights and suggestions that materially improved the quality of this volume.

Lastly, I offer a special tribute to my wife Donna-Belle, who carried out most of the research for this book and who devoted as much time to the project as did I.

James L. Garvin
Research Curator

This map of the center of Portsmouth was excerpted from that published by Charles W. Brewster in 1850, from the original surveys directed by Civil Engineer H.F. Walling.

NOBLES ISLAND
PORTLAND SACO
BADGER'S ISLAND
FERNALD & PETTIGREW'S SHIPYARD
PART OF KITTERY
School
PISCATAQ
NORTH MILL POND
SOUTH MILL POND
3
ELM STREET
NORTH CEMETERY
GEO. RAYNE'S SHIP YARD
TIMBER DOCK
Sawmill Gristmill
Franklin School
Portsmouth Steam Mill
Sagamore Mill
Jail
CONCORD RAILROAD
MARKET SQUARE
Brick Market
Franklin House
Temple
South Church
Court House
Universalist Church
Pleasant St. Bap Church
Old South Church
Point of Graves
Iron Works
Mariners House
DOCK
Franklin Iron Foundry
Haven School
Arsenal
ROPEWALK
Grist Mill
MARKET ST.
BOW ST.
HIGH ST.
CONGRESS
STATE ST.
COURT
ISLINGTON
MIDDLE
AUBURN
SUMMER
NEWCASTLE ST.
WASHINGTON
PLEASANT
HANOVER
VAUGHAN
DEER
BRIDGE
ROCK
MARLBOROUGH
HANCOCK ST.
GATES
HOWARD ST.
GARDNER ST.
PICKERING ST.
SALTER ST.
PRAY ST.
SOUTH SCHOOL ST.
BLOSSOM ST.
CABOT
WINTER
CHATHAM ST.
DOVER
SALEM
MAC DONOUGH
LIME
PENN
CORNWALL
ANTHONY
AUSTIN
MADISON
CASS
Bridge Wharf
Frasts Wharf
Exchange Wharf
Portsmouth Pier Company's Wharves
Commercial Wharf
Long Wharf
Union Wharf
Wendells Wh.
Central Wh.
Marine Railway

Photographer Lafayette V. Newell, self-portrait made about 1880. (Patch Collection)

Introduction

EARLY PHOTOGRAPHY IN PORTSMOUTH

When the process of photography was first proclaimed to an unprepared public in 1839, the announcement was greeted with incredulity. How could it be possible to fix forever the fleeting image cast by a lens? The immediate reaction of the world, which recognized only the marvelous technical advance of the process, was summed up by the French artist Paul Delaroche: "Painting is dead from this day." Perhaps no one at the time realized that the science of photography would offer man at least the partial realization of a cherished dream: the ability to travel through time. True, this time-travel is limited to the period between the mid-1800s and the present, but even this modest capability is exhilarating and endlessly fascinating, as the following photographs of one small locale amply suggest.

The special quality that permits us to use the photograph as a window into the past is the same quality against which art critics have inveighed: the photograph is "merely" a mechanically and chemically produced record of a specific moment in time. Human judgment plays only a small part in deciding which details of the scene before the camera's lens will be recorded, especially in these matter-of-fact early views. The lens is ravenous and undiscriminating; it records everything. While such a complete and objective record may not be "art," it is indeed history. And the photographer, perhaps unwittingly, is the historian. Moreover, he is a historian of great power, for he can convey us visually as well as mentally into the past, to see with our own eyes not only the true aspect of events before our time, but likewise every nuance and detail of those events, from the young spring leaves on the trees to the rutted mud in the streets.

The photographer also possesses a power unimagined by any other historian: he renders trivial and everyday events both interesting and significant. By so doing, he performs a great service to those who wish to see the past as it really was. What would once have passed "below the level of historical scrutiny" is now frozen on glass for the present and the future to ponder.

Who, then, were the photographers who left the rich heritage that spreads itself before us on these pages? Although it has seldom been possible to credit specific photographs to specific men, the two individuals who recorded most of the following views were Lafayette V. Newell and Caleb S. Gurney, both of whom have largely been forgotten except by a few local antiquarians. Newell and Gurney were active from the 1870s until just after 1900. Before them came earlier pioneers whose contributions deserve brief mention.

In January, 1839, Louis Jacques Mandé Daguerre, a French artist, astonished the world by announcing his development of the first successful photographic process. The daguerreotype, named for its inventor, recorded the image cast by a camera lens on a sensitized plate of silver-coated copper. The image so obtained was reversed from right to left, was clearly visible only when seen in reflected light that reduced the glare of the silvered plate, and required both a long camera exposure and an elaborate procedure for preparing and developing the plate. Nevertheless, the daguerreotype, perfected only after laborious experimentation between 1825 and 1839, provided a photograph of extreme sharpness and, given proper care, of great permanence.

On June 15, 1839, the French government purchased the secret of Daguerre's process from its inventor. France's political and scientific leaders generously arranged to have the technique described to the public so that experimenters everywhere could benefit from the incredible discovery. On August 19, 1839, the French Academy of Sciences revealed the details of Daguerre's process to an eager audience, and soon published a description of the photographic technique.

The published description first arrived in the United States on September 20, 1839, when the *British Queen*, an English express steam packet, docked in New York. From that date, it theoretically became possible for American experimenters to begin making photographs, although only those who possessed an unusual degree of skill and wealth were actually able to acquire the expensive cameras and elaborate chemical apparatus necessary to produce the daguerreotype.

Surprisingly, however, Portsmouth was one of the first towns in New England in which photographs were successfully made. Barely six months after the *British Queen* docked in New York, a forty-three-year-old Portsmouth "professor of painting," Samuel P. Long, succeeded in making at least one photograph. On February 22, 1840, the *Portsmouth Journal* excitedly described Long's experiment:

> The wonderful art of preparing a process for nature to transfer landscapes in miniature upon a permanent plate, merely by the operation of rays of light, is decidedly the greatest discovery of our age. When the first account was published, a few months since, we regarded it as a hoax: but are now convinced, from an actual examination of a sketch from our ingenious townsman, SAMUEL P. LONG, Esq. The sketch is taken of the scenery in the neighborhood of the Universalist Church in this town, from Auburn Street. The church at that distance is delineated at about an inch in width, but so perfectly that even the sashes of the pulpit window can be plainly seen. An intervening elm tree, with all its naked limbs and most minute twigs, is perfectly delineated. We can give no idea by a description. Take the most finished engraving in our Annuals made in dark shades on steel, and you can form some idea of the sketch, but not of its perfection . . . .

Although the Portsmouth newspaper referred to Long as "in fact the first successful experimenter in New-England," others in Boston had actually preceded the Portsmouth artist in producing daguerreotypes. Still, Long was indeed a pioneer. On the same date that Long's success was announced to the citizens of Portsmouth, the *Journal* also described the first public demonstration in New York by François Gouraud, Daguerre's friend and pupil, who had arrived in America aboard the *British Queen*.

More astonishing (and perhaps colored a bit by local pride) were the accolades that the *Journal* accorded Long after his own public demonstration in his Portsmouth Academy classroom on March 12, 1840. "The apparatus of Mr. L. is of the first order, and his

"Shooting a deserter at Point Lookout, Maryland, 1863," *from an early paper print made by Lafayette V. Newell.* (Patch Collection)

illustrations of the beauty of the art are fine," announced the newspaper. "Those who have seen both, readily proclaim Mr. L.'s productions superior to Gouraud's, which are now exhibiting in Boston." This was high praise indeed, considering that Gouraud is known to have exhibited not only his own work, but also photographs made by Daguerre himself.

The wondrous new art inspired public patronage. Within a decade, other photographers had established commercial studios in Portsmouth. In January of 1849, the *Journal* announced the moving of "Ham's Daguerrean Gallery" from Congress Hall to S. Ham's building opposite the Mansion House Hotel on Congress Street. By the end of 1850, Albert Gregory (1815-1887), one of Portsmouth's finest early photographers, had a studio at 33 Congress Street.

Once a building was converted for use as a photographic studio by the installation of large windows and sky-lights, it was often used by a number of photographers in succession. A case in point is 8 Daniel Street, which was used for photographic rooms at least as early as 1851 when the "daguerrean" Francis M. Danielson had his studio there. By 1853, "Mr. Salen's Daguerrean Atelier" was established at the same address. In 1861, the Davis Brothers, "Daguerrean artists," were at 8 Daniel Street, followed in 1864 by Carl Meinerth, in 1869 by William T. Clark, and in 1873 by Mark J. Hall. The studio at 33 Congress Street, first occupied by Albert Gregory, had a similar history.

One of the most colorful and revealing advertisements of the early daguerreotypists began to appear in the *Portsmouth Journal* in June, 1853:

> City Daguerreotype Room.
> Friends, Citizens and Strangers, all, who are desirous to procure a true and faithful LIKENESS, beautifully finished, please call at Mr. SALEN'S DAGUERREAN ATELIER, No. 8 Daniel street, and examine his specimens.
>
> Sick and deceased persons taken at their residences.

Mr. Salen, whose declamatory style of advertising was characteristic of the period, and especially of photographers of the period, remained in town only a short while, probably leaving when the trade in "likenesses" began to taper off. The last sentence of Salen's notice is particularly interesting, as it mentions one function of the early photographer that seems both morbid and poignant to the modern mind. In an age when portraits were seldom made, a person's death frequently brought his relatives to the shocking realization that they possessed no visual record of the deceased. Thus, portraits of the dead, and especially of dead children, were particularly common in these early years.

In 1854, the Bostonian James A. Cutting developed a method for fixing a photographic image on a sensitized coating on a glass plate. This form of photograph possessed most of the advantages of the daguerreotype, but was easier to view because the glass surface reflected less glare than the polished silver surface of the earlier invention. This new photographic form became known as the ambrotype (the term is believed to be derived from the Greek

Photographic studio of Lafayette V. Newell in the upper floors of the Peduzzi Building, northwest corner of Congress and High streets (demolished 1890). Note the large window and skylight for illumination. (Patch Collection)

word for immortality, which may give some idea of the fascination with which people of the day viewed the process). Like the daguerreotype, the ambrotype permitted only a single picture for each camera exposure. No intermediate master negative, of the sort familiar today, was produced to permit making subsequent prints.

Ambrotype photography quickly eclipsed the former popularity of the daguerreotype, becoming predominant in 1856 and 1857. Thus, it is not surprising to find that at least one ambrotype studio was flourishing in the Piscataqua region during this period. The firm of G.B. and G.E. Sawyer of Salmon Falls, New Hampshire, was making ambrotypes at least as early as 1857. On some occasions, at least, the Sawyers are known to have made outdoor photographs of buildings and notable scenes—a rather rare undertaking with this type of photography.

The ambrotype, in its turn, was quickly supplanted after 1857 by the increasing perfection of the photographic process that has remained standard up to the present day. Known as the collodion process, this technique produces pictures in two stages. In the first stage, a plate of glass (or flexible plastic in modern cameras) which has been coated with light-sensitive chemicals is exposed to the image cast by the lens in the camera. Through a type of chemical legerdemain similar to that used in earlier photography, this image is permanently fixed on the plate. The plate is then a "negative," from which positive prints, like all of those seen in this book, can be produced on light-sensitive paper. From a single negative, innumerable paper prints can subsequently be made.

Portsmouth did not have to wait long for the appearance of practitioners of the new photographic art. The pioneering Albert Gregory, who had appeared about 1850 as one of Portsmouth's first daguerreotypists, was among the first to produce paper prints. His classic studies of the U.S.S. *Constitution* at the Navy Yard, printed on paper and often pasted to mats with captions describing the event, were made in 1858. Gregory must have made many other collodion-process photographs during the same period.

In 1861, two brothers, Lewis G. Davis (1833-1909) and Charles Davis (1836-1911), formed an enduring partnership under the name "Davis Brothers." Although the Davises began their work rather late in the history of photographic evolution, they continued to offer both daguerreotypes and ambrotypes to Portsmouth customers perhaps not sufficiently sophisticated to realize that both these media were already outmoded in stylish urban centers. The Davises were also equipped, however, to utilize the new collodion process. In 1864, they advertised:

> Large size photographs, Plain India Ink, and colored in Oil or Water Colors, taken from life, or copied from old pictures, magnified to any size desired, and warranted to give satisfaction. Cartes de Visite in Vignette and all other styles. Ambrotypes taken and every kind of Photographic work done in the best style of the art.

Although the Davises were still producing ambrotypes for their more conservative clientele, they were also

Photographer Caleb Stevens Gurney; self-portrait made about 1885. (Courtesy of Mrs. Ethel C. Storer)

offering one of the most fashionable types of photographs, the *carte de visite* or card photograph. These once-popular paper prints, intended especially for exchange among friends and for inclusion in the ubiquitous family album, measured about 2⅛" by 3½", and were mounted on cards that were slightly larger. The subject was usually shown full-length in a standing posture, often with an ornate and pretentious painted background, although the "vignette" style, advertised by the Davises, involved the gradual fading-out of the picture to leave only a bust portrait of the subject.

The Davis Brothers also found a very lucrative and long-lived business in the production of another photographic form, the stereoscope slide. Some of the earliest Portsmouth photographs that survive today are Davis stereographs.

Almost everyone is familiar with the stereoscope or, as it is often incorrectly called, the "stereopticon." It is the device through which one looks at two apparently identical photographs and sees a single image which is astounding in its three-dimensionality. The form of stereoscope most readily recognized today was invented in 1859 by the versatile American physician and man of letters, Oliver Wendell Holmes. The "Holmes stereoscope" consists of a formed face-piece with two lenses, a projecting wooden rail with a sliding holder for the "stereograph" (a card bearing two paper photographs mounted side by side), and a handle or table pedestal beneath. The two apparently identical photographs on the card are actually slightly different, having been taken by a double-lens camera. The distance between the camera lenses, about 2.5 inches, approximates the distance between the eyes of man. When the viewer observes the two different images on the stereograph through the stereoscope, the brain fuses the two images into one. This single blended mental image has the quality of three-dimensionality, exactly as do the images seen in nature by human eyes.

The three-dimensional stereoscope image is so compelling in its illusion of reality and so endlessly fascinating in its revelation of depth and detail that collecting foreign and domestic stereographs became a major pastime after the mid-nineteenth century. At the very beginning of their partnership, the Davis brothers found that they had competition in the Portsmouth stereograph business. In 1861, the *Portsmouth Chronicle* announced:

> Mr. Meinerth has recently taken quite a large series of views, for the stereoscope, of our principal streets, public buildings, private residences, etc., and has been eminently successful. They are admirably executed and our citizens would only consult their own interests should they obtain of him pictures of places and scenes endeared to them by long acquaintance and hallowed by many pleasing remembrances . . . .

Carl Meinerth had begun to advertise his services as a teacher of drawing and music in the *Portsmouth Journal* of 1853. He continued these occupations throughout the fifties, but had established "Photograph and Ambrotype Rooms" at 8 Daniel Street at least as early as 1864. Meinerth remained active in Portsmouth as a photographer for only a few years, moving to New-

Interior of John W. Newell's studio, with a display of matted and framed historic photographs. (Patch Collection)

buryport after the mid-sixties. A few of his stereographs and card photographs survive today in private hands.

Portsmouth required more than stereoscope slides and *cartes de visite* to supply its photographic needs, however. Nearly all of the pictures on the following pages were reproduced from 5- by 7-inch or 8- by 10-inch glass plate negatives, and were made to record special events. Prints from such negatives, if sold to the public, were usually mounted on large neutral-toned cardboard mats, suitable for framing. It is evident that Portsmouth required a photographer who was prepared to execute such work and to function much in the manner of the present-day commercial photographer, meeting the increasingly diverse needs of an increasingly photograph-conscious community.

Such a man appeared in the energetic person of Lafayette V. Newell (1833-1914). Born in Barnstead, New Hampshire, Newell was one of thirteen children of a prominent farmer. He attended district school in Barnstead and demonstrated an unusual talent at penmanship. Deciding to use his skill to good advantage, he traveled to Concord in 1854 and began to teach penmanship and to write address cards with a flowing script resembling copperplate engraving.

In 1856, Newell began to work as a photographer in Concord. After six months he came to Portsmouth, where he again engaged in the teaching of calligraphy, worked as a bookkeeper for the brewer John Swindell, and briefly ran an oyster saloon. At the beginning of the Civil War, Newell returned to Concord and went into partnership with the Baker brothers' daguerreotype firm.

Although Newell has never been listed among the limited number of photographers who recorded the Civil War, he was in fact one of this select fraternity. In 1862, at the solicitation of his twin brother Albert M. Newell (a member of the Twelfth New Hampshire Volunteers), Newell went to Point Lookout, Maryland, where the Fifth, Sixth, and Twelfth New Hampshire Regiments were guarding 25,000 Confederate prisoners.

Newell purchased lumber for a gallery in Baltimore. This material was transported to Point Lookout, a distance of about one hundred miles, and within seven days the photographer had constructed a twelve by twenty-five-foot studio. Business was brisk, and Newell made hundreds of portraits of both Union and Confederate officers and men, at one time employing a rebel prisoner as an assistant. Newell remained at Point Lookout throughout most of the war's duration. One of the few scenes surviving from that period in his life is the somber photograph reproduced here, which records the execution of a deserter in 1863.

When Newell returned to Portsmouth, he may have felt that he could not succeed as a photographer in competition with the Davis Brothers and other cameramen who appeared in town during the 1860s and early 1870s. In any case, he worked as a partner in the grocery firm of his father-in-law, John E. Rider, storing his Point Lookout negatives in the store's attic. At some undetermined time, vandals broke open the two large trunks in which the priceless negatives were stored, and destroyed most of the collection. The print reproduced here is therefore doubly rare.

By the late seventies, however, Newell re-commenced his occupation as photographer. His services found an increasing demand, not only in the studio or in the streets of Portsmouth, but at the Navy Yard as well. Those photographs on the following pages which can be identified as Newell's amply attest to his skill as an artist and technician, and to his importance as a photographic historian.

The name of Caleb Stevens Gurney (1848-1924) is familiar to every devotee of Portsmouth's history, for Gurney was the author of the unique and valuable photographic chronicle, *Portsmouth . . . Historic and Picturesque* (1902). Beyond this fact, however, few people now recall anything of this highly colorful and once well-known figure, whose camera supplied most of the architectural photographs in this volume.

Gurney was born in Hebron, Maine, and was educated at Hebron Academy. His interest in photography must have begun by the time he was twenty, for in 1871, when he was twenty-three, he purchased a photographic business from Dimon Perry of Mechanic Falls.

Gurney was not destined to remain permanently in any single place, however. About 1880, he moved to Kennebunk, Maine, where he resumed his photographic business. The accompanying self-portrait, probably made around 1885, attests to his skill as a photographer. The picture also shows that Gurney was well aware of the fashion of the times, for the original is an example of the then-popular "cabinet portrait"—a paper picture measuring 4 by 5¼ inches and mounted on a somewhat larger card in the manner of the earlier and smaller *cartes de visite.*

Gurney's sister-in-law married William E. Storer, whose family owned the shoe factory at Kennebunk and opened the Portsmouth Shoe Company in 1886. This situation brought Gurney to Portsmouth in 1888 not as a photographer, but as shipping clerk of the shoe factory. Shortly after 1890, however, Gurney returned to the photograph business as proprietor of the "Acme Portrait Company," and, after 1897, as owner of the "Company International de Bellas Artes." Evidence suggests that this latter venture took the enterprising photographer to South America at least once.

Gurney reserved some of his abundant energy for projects closer to home, however. By 1900 or earlier, he began a systematic program of recording most of Portsmouth's early buildings for his forthcoming book, at the same time gathering historical information and collecting reminiscences of the city's most aged men. The publication of *Portsmouth . . . Historic and Picturesque* in 1902 was a milestone in local history; neither before nor since has a photographer compiled so complete a record of the city's architectural and scenic wealth. The scope of Gurney's undertaking, however, resulted in his pictures being reduced greatly for printing. Many of Gurney's original negatives were used in the preparation of the present volume, and here, for the first time, the reader may see this pioneering photographer's pictures with the size and clarity they deserve.

Gurney's restless nature soon impelled him toward other enterprises. Between 1905 and 1910 he emerged as the president of the "Gurney Ball Joint Umbrella Company"—which, despite the somewhat uncharacteristic nature of the business for a photographer and author, actually did produce an umbrella with certain superiorities even to present-day models. About 1910, Gurney moved to Boston, where he spent the remainder of his life in various pursuits, including further photographic work.

The reader may wonder how the priceless negatives of the early photographers were transmitted down to the present day. Considering the fragile, perishable nature of glass plate negatives, as well as the fact that the pictures could only (until recently) have been regarded as old-fashioned, it is a miracle indeed that so many early negatives survive in reproducible condition.

Their survival may be attributed to the unusual care and historical insight of a few men. Many of Newell's negatives passed to his son, John William Newell (1867-1931), who had worked with his father throughout the latter's lifetime. The younger Newell was not only a photographer himself, but a collector of rare and early photographs, as the accompanying view of his studio attests. It is likely that he acquired a number of negatives that were taken by early photographers other than his father.

After the younger Newell died as a result of an automobile accident, his collection came into the hands of the noted antique dealer Charles H. Stewart, along with most of Caleb Gurney's negatives. After Stewart's death, the collection was acquired by Garland W. Patch (1905-1971). Although Patch worked most of his life as a Navy Yard welder, his real love was in antiquarian research and he was for many years the curator of the Thomas Bailey Aldrich Memorial and the Portsmouth Athenaeum. He eventually acquired negatives made by other pioneering photographers, and took delight in studying and cataloguing this rich heritage. He sold his entire collection to Strawbery Banke, Inc., in 1970. Pictures from the Patch Collection constitute the majority of those used in this book.

Another major figure in the conservation of Portsmouth's photographic legacy was Walter Chesley Staples (1879-1957). During his early life, Staples worked as a blueprinter, and then became a commercial photographer, taking several of the later pictures reproduced in this volume. More important, he worked for many years as a photographer at the Navy Yard. In this capacity, Staples had access to a number of early photographs, some originally taken by Lafayette V. Newell, that had never found their way into the Patch Collection. Like John Newell, Staples was keenly interested in the preservation of these early pictures, and made copy negatives of many. After his death, Staples' collection passed to his son, Eliot A. Staples, who in turn gave it to the *Portsmouth Herald*. The *Herald* donated the collection to Strawbery Banke, Inc., in 1972.

It is no accident, then, that the reader is able to step back in time fifty, seventy-five or a hundred years at the turning of a page. It is the result of years of work by a number of photographers who loved their region, and of decades of patient and largely unappreciated care by collectors and antiquarians who cherished the heritage that passed into their stewardship. But for these men, the reader would remain locked in the narrowest prison that can confine mankind—the prison of the present moment.

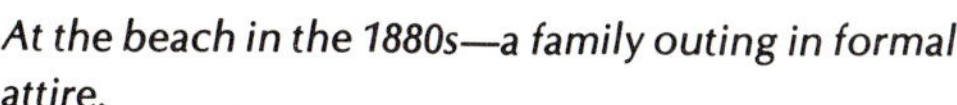

At the beach in the 1880s—a family outing in formal attire.

The Urban Setting

1. The first settlers on the site of present-day Portsmouth found three tidal creeks around which they built their structures. The middle waterway, the smallest, became the site for the "Great House," a large communal dwelling erected by the newcomers after 1630. Later in the seventeenth and eighteenth centuries, the shores of this tidal inlet became more and more densely crowded with dwellings, shops, and warehouses. During the 1800s the area suffered an economic and social decline, and the ancient creek became known by the whimsical name, "Puddle Dock." By the late nineteenth century, the city received complaints of the noxious odors arising from the flats of the dock, and between 1899 and 1907 the basin was filled with some 25,000 cubic yards of ashes and debris.

This photograph, probably dating from about 1899, records the last days of Puddle Dock. In the left foreground, at the foot of Whidden Place, is an omen of things to come—a pile of tin cans and refuse that begin to encroach on the mud flats.

At the far left is the elevated wooden tank of a pumping station for filling street sprinkling wagons. The long building beyond this began its existence about 1877 as a boiler shop, and became a tenement about 1893 after serving for a time as a stable. In the center of the photograph is the Liberty Pole at Liberty Bridge, and just to the right of the bridge span may be seen part of an old pump and spar shop. In the right background, the steep roof of the central-chimney Wentworth House (c. 1695), survivor of the first phases of settlement along the creek, towers over its more modern neighbors. The clerestory roof in front of the Wentworth House belongs to an old smokehouse once used to cure fish. The shed- and gable-roofed buildings attached to it were fish warehouses.

A few years after this photograph was made, a broad avenue was extended directly from the camera's vantage-point to Liberty Bridge, and the old buildings began to disappear. By the 1930s the area was filled with junkyards and tenement houses. These were removed by urban renewal in 1963 and 1964, and today the neighborhood is administered by Strawbery Banke, Inc., which one day will excavate the old waterway. Sadly, however, not a single building seen in this photograph remains.

Staples-Herald Collection

2. "The view you get looking across Liberty Bridge, Water Street, is probably the same in every respect that presented itself to the eyes of the town folk a century ago." Thus wrote Thomas Bailey Aldrich in 1874, close to the time this stereoscope slide was made. At the crest of the road is Liberty Bridge, first thrown across the outlet of the Puddle Dock waterway in 1731.

The white building on the left was a grocery store, while those on the right-hand side of the street were used as stables, warehouses, and dwellings. Behind the flagpole may be seen a diminutive shed-roofed fish store, almost indistinguishable from the larger building behind it.

This photograph provides almost the only visual record of the 1824 Liberty Pole, which was replaced by a taller flagstaff in 1899. The 1824 pole was erected with great ceremony and celebration on July 4 to commemorate the original unfurling of a banner in 1766 to protest the Stamp Act. Atop the old eighty-five-foot pole may be seen a forty-three-inch wooden eagle and a liberty cap finial said to have been carved by Laban S. Beecher of Boston. Near the base of the pole, just above the roof of the building in the background, is a carved wooden shield made in 1857 by Benjamin A. Gleason and Joseph Henderson, ship and ornamental carvers of 34 Bow Street, Portsmouth. Both of these relics have been carefully preserved and are mounted on the present Liberty Pole.

2

Patch Collection

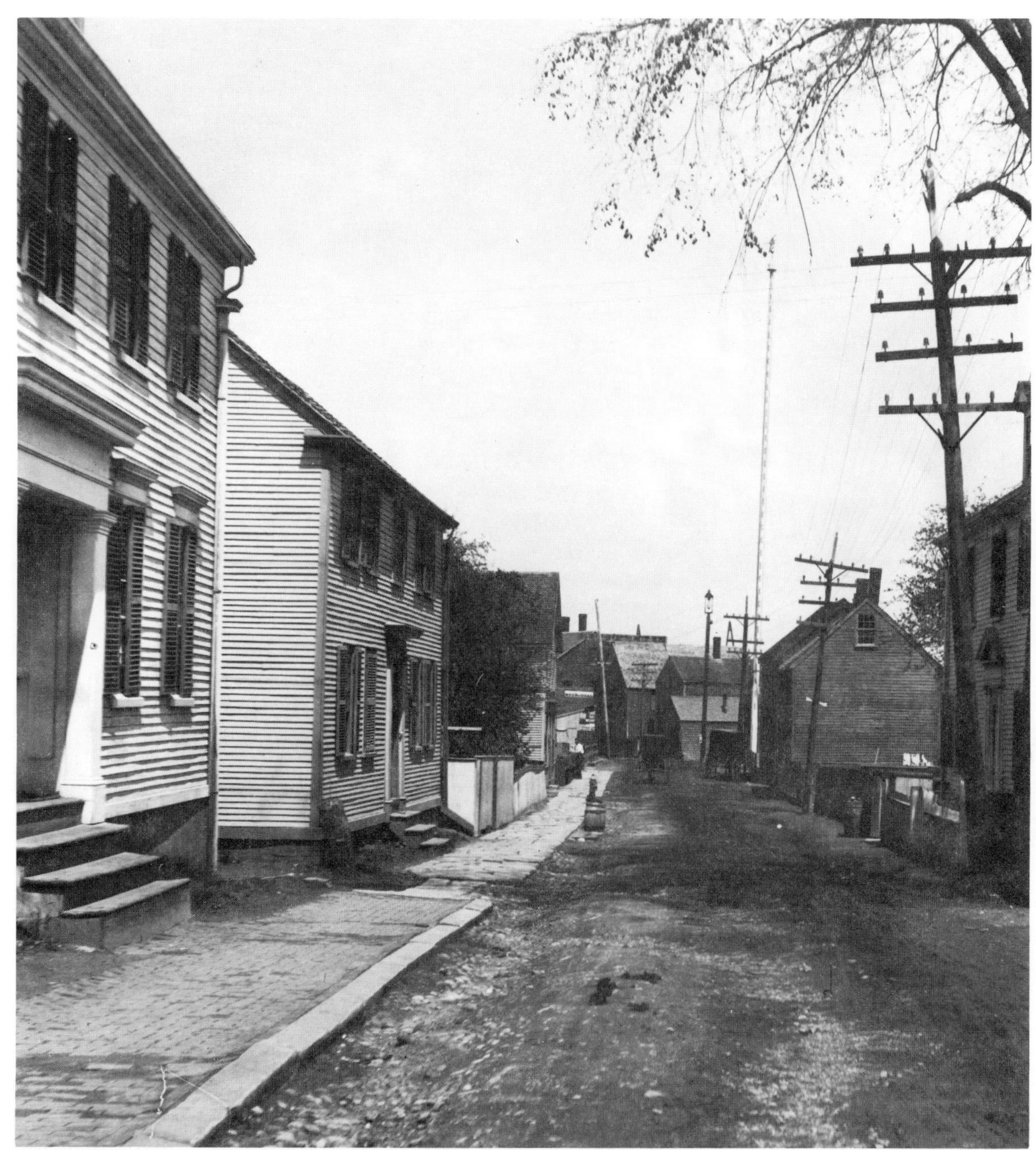

3. By 1900, Water Street had begun to change its appearance. The 1824 Liberty Pole had been replaced in 1899 by a 110-foot staff of Oregon pine, and old Puddle Dock was steadily being filled in. The street had reached the height of its most infamous and colorful era as well: it had become Portsmouth's chief red-light district, and its northern end was crowded with saloons, dance halls, and boarding houses. This peaceful scene belies the neighborhood's night-time activities, which resulted in several murders and innumerable brawls between sailors, marines, and local toughs, and which have provided material for hundreds of Portsmouth legends in the more peaceful years since.

3 *Patch Collection*

4. In 1802, a devastating fire swept through the central part of Portsmouth. "The whole beauty of the town is gone! is gone!!" lamented the *New-Hampshire Gazette*; but even as the debris was being cleared a group of influential citizens was planning to erect "handsome Brick Buildings" on the burnt-over tract. The result of their plans is suggested in this photograph of Market Square in 1870. In the center is the striking Portsmouth Athenaeum, completed in 1805 as the office of the New Hampshire Fire and Marine Insurance Company. Its first-floor reading-room, lighted by the splendid arched windows and doorway, was once the "subscription room" of the insurance office. Here, merchants, mariners, and businessmen met to discuss the news of ship arrivals and departures. They would agree on underwriting part of the risk on vessels or buildings needing marine and fire insurance. The building has been the home of the Athenaeum since 1823.

Originally, the Athenaeum was the center of a unified architectural composition, but the Haven Block, on the right, had already been altered when this photograph was taken. When the 234-foot row of buildings was first constructed, however, all structures had not only shared the marble string-courses seen on the block to the left, but had also been covered with flat roofs of pine pitch and gravel—a daring experiment in 1805.

Patch Collection

5. Congress Street in 1870 presented a scene of tranquillity that has been unknown for the past half century. From Fleet Street westward, the boulevard was still largely residential, its colonial, post-Revolutionary and Victorian buildings producing an effect of dignified harmony. The North Church steeple towers above Market Square in the background. Today, the brick, bow-front building on the right side of the street is the Kearsarge Hotel.

Patch Collection

6. Parking problems are not unique to the twentieth century, as this view of Congress Street between 1890 and 1895 amply proves. Once a fine residential area, upper Congress Street was overwhelmed by commercial interests after the Civil War. On the extreme left, occupied by Frank W. Rice's oyster house, stands the venerable dwelling of Hunking Wentworth, a zealous Revolutionary patriot who was at the same time Chairman of the Committee of Safety and uncle of the Royal Governor! The large wooden structure beyond is the Rev. Nathaniel Rogers House, built in 1705 for the minister of the North Church and raised about ten feet from its foundation in 1872 to provide room for stores beneath. Most of the remaining structures are Victorian and were almost new when this photograph was made. Many of them have since given way to more modern buildings.

Photograph by Newell and Company; Patch Collection

6

7

7. Seldom does a scene convey the essence of nineteenth century commerce as well as does this photograph of Bow Street about 1881. The unpaved road, the cobblestone crosswalk in the foreground, the oxcart awaiting its load, the wagons unhitched in the street, the towering masts of the schooner tied up at the wharves behind the unbroken row of commercial structures—these elements of Portsmouth life have vanished in less than a century.

At the time this photograph was made, number 16 Bow Street was occupied by Josiah S. James, flour and grain merchant. Next door was the "small beer" manufactory of Charles E. Boynton. The same building had been occupied twenty years earlier by Charles E. Peck, a carriage and sleigh manufacturer, whose painted advertisement had not yet weathered away. Beyond Boynton's was a storehouse with all but its upper windows securely shuttered. Next to the Eldridge Brewery Office were wooden buildings used as a residence and as carpenter and joiner shops. The brick building at the far right was a cod-liver-oil manufactory. On the right, up the hill from John F. Shillaber's gunsmithing establishment, is the blacksmith and horseshoeing shop of George G. Wendell, a fact which explains the horseless wagons that crowd about its door.

Patch Collection

8. The streets of Portsmouth, like those of many a country town, were once "rolled" after heavy snow storms to provide a good surface for sleighs and pungs. This stereoscope slide of 1858 records no less than eight span of oxen pulling a roller across the intersection of State and Pleasant streets. The teams are stopped directly abreast of the then-new granite Custom House (out of the picture on the right) which was just beginning to rise from its cellar in the winter of '58. On the other side of Pleasant Street may be seen the shop of James H. Head, who sold books, music, stationery, and wallpapers; the offices of the New Hampshire National Bank; the "Daguerrean Gallery" of the Davis brothers (who made this photograph); the office of C.N. Shaw and Company, milliners; and, on the other side of State Street, the apothecary store of Joseph H. Thacher.

Patch Collection

8

9

10

9. In March, 1671, Captain John Pickering II agreed that the town should "have full liberty to enclose about half an acre upon the neck of land . . . where the people have been wont to be buried, which land shall be impropriated forever unto the use of a burying place." This half-acre lot, Portsmouth's oldest cemetery, has long been known by the picturesque name of "Point of Graves." It is located where the waters of old Puddle Dock once merged with the turbulent current of the main river.

Patch Collection

10. The story of large families and early death is told in this double stone at the Point of Graves. Two sisters—one of whom had already buried her first husband and married again, and one of whom had yet to marry—lie beneath a single gravestone. In 1697, the year after the youngest girl died, their father, Major Charles Frost, was ambushed and killed by Indians while returning from church. The settlers of the Piscataqua did not need the *New England Primer's* reminder that "From Death's Arrest No Age is Free."

Patch Collection

11. Closely spaced wooden dwellings on narrow treeless streets—this is the essence of Portsmouth's old South End. The ancient gambrel-roofed dwelling, which even as early as 1870 seemed to be settling slowly onto its site atop Meeting House Hill, may have been built earlier than its reputed date of 1732. The house was constructed in two stages, the side on the right being the earlier half. Evidence suggests that the house had a gable roof before it was enlarged to its present form. The right-hand portion is notable for having two massive summer beams supporting the second floor. In the late eighteenth and early nineteenth centuries, the house was occupied by the venerable Captain Daniel Fernald, who could recall a time when the waters of Puddle Dock flowed across Pleasant Street to merge with those of the South Mill Pond at high tide.

The public pump in the foreground stood on the crest of Meeting House Hill until after 1900. The well beneath it, though now disused, still exists.

Patch Collection

11

12. The ancient but nearly forgotten custom of converting the lower rooms of dwellings into small shops is perfectly illustrated in this photograph from about 1875. The house once stood at the corner of Sheafe and Chapel streets. The shop in the left-hand room may possibly have been used by James Jamison, a baker who occupied the building in the 1870s. Much of the ancient business district, destroyed in the great fires of 1802, 1804, and 1813, was made up of wooden dwellings with their lower floors adapted as shops, and recent investigations in the early South End have shown that the practice was common in that section also.

Patch Collection

12

13

13. This was Thomas Bailey Aldrich's boyhood home and was transformed into the "Nutter House" in his classic *The Story of a Bad Boy,* published in 1868. In 1877, the house became an orphanage, and between 1884 and 1895 it served as the Portsmouth hospital. This photograph, made about 1900, shows the building in use as a private two-family residence. On June 30, 1908, it was dedicated as the Thomas Bailey Aldrich Memorial, one of the first houses in America to be restored to its appearance at a specific time in its past.

On the left may be seen a now-destroyed sidewalk, paved with flagstones of stratified granite, brought eleven miles downriver from Durham. In his 1801 "Century Sermon," the Rev. Timothy Alden remarked, "We have but one street entirely paved. In the course of a few years, however, one side of most of our streets has been paved with very nice flat stones brought from Durham, in such a manner that two or three persons can conveniently walk abreast." Before the streets were covered with cobblestones or macadam, granite crosswalks, like that extending from the Aldrich House door, conveyed pedestrians safely across a sea of springtime mud.

Patch Collection

14. Until the turn of the twentieth century, Pleasant Street in Portsmouth was one of the great thoroughfares in the United States, presenting a distinguished array of fine architectural examples ranging in date from the mid-1700s to the early 1800s. Of the three large houses seen in this photograph from about 1898, only one, the Wendell House on the right, has survived.

The three-story house is said to have been built as a gambrel-roofed dwelling shortly after 1760. It was the home of the Rev. Dr. Samuel Haven, pastor of the South Church, and was the birthplace of his large family of prosperous children. The old building was remodelled into a three-story house shortly after 1800, when such dwellings were in vogue. In 1898, the Haven House was dismantled and its gardens became the nucleus of the present Haven Park.

During the Revolution, Dr. Haven operated a manufactory for producing saltpetre (a component of gunpowder) to the north of his house. On this site in 1799 the Welsh merchant Edward Parry erected the hip-roofed house seen in the center of this photograph. The Parry House, although superficially nearly a duplicate of the earlier Wendell House at the right, had interior trim of a more modern early Federal style. This beautiful house was moved to Marginal Road (Parrott Avenue) on the north shore of the nearby mill pond about 1900, its superb garden becoming part of Haven Park. The house deteriorated on its new site and was finally demolished in 1941.

The Wendell House was built about 1789 by Jeremiah Hill. It was occupied in 1814 by Joshua Haven, a member of the once-numerous and prominent, but now extinct, Portsmouth family. Haven left the house in 1816 to occupy a superb brick mansion on Islington Street built by Jonathan Folsom—the present Knights of Columbus building. Thereafter, the Pleasant Street house has been owned continuously by members of the Wendell family.

Staples-Herald Collection

14

15. After their first formal organization in Portsmouth in 1777, the Universalist Society met in several buildings including the meeting houses of other sects. In 1784, they erected their first meeting house on the west side of Vaughan Street. By 1807, however, the society had grown in membership and prosperity to the point that many church members desired to erect a new and larger meeting house. As was a common practice in those days, a group of seventy men contracted to build the new structure at their own risk and expense, and in return the society agreed that the income from the sale of the pews in the meeting house should become the property of this group as its reimbursement.

A plan was prepared for the new building, possibly by the builder-architect James Nutter. Nutter was an active member of the Universalist Church at the time, and was then engaged as the master joiner on the new St. John's Church. The design of the building was based upon three sources: a plate from Asher Benjamin's newly-published architectural guidebook, *The American Builder's Companion;* the facade of Bradbury Johnson's Portsmouth Athenaeum; and the 1801 Unitarian meeting house in Newburyport. The latter not only supplied the inspiration for the tower and lantern of the Portsmouth building, but was "fixed upon as the standard as to materials and workmanship."

A site was acquired on Pleasant Street, nearly opposite the John Langdon mansion, and work was begun in March, 1807. The structure, which was superbly fashioned of wood, was completed by the following December, and was described at its dedication as the largest and finest church edifice in New Hampshire. Exclusive of its foundation and bell, the structure cost $10,500. The major contractors were Asa Robinson and

15

Samuel Cofran of Pembroke, New Hampshire. The Universalist Church contributed greatly to the beauty of Portsmouth, and helped to make Pleasant Street one of the most beautiful thoroughfares in America. Tragically, the building burned on March 28, 1896.

Patch Collection

16. From an early time, the Portsmouth Athenaeum reading room served as a meeting place for many of the prominent men of the town. So familiar did their gathered faces become that they were jestingly referred to as "The Athenaeum Boys"—a name by which this photograph, taken in 1891, has always been identified.

Patch Collection

17. Before the age of power machinery, human and animal muscle did the nation's work. When the main sewer line was laid in Pleasant Street in the nineties, it took this gang of over one hundred men, armed with picks and shovels, to do the job. Less than seventy years later a crew of fewer than ten men with a back-hoe followed the same route with a still larger pipe in a fraction of the time.

The men are seated on the steps of the 1807 Universalist Church, which burned in 1896. The number of greybeards in the group shows that hard labor was not reserved for young men alone, and that retirement was often impossible for the workingman. An interesting commentary on the universality of the hat in the nineteenth century is provided by the fact that only six members of the group lack some form of headgear.

Patch Collection

16

17

18. Many residents of New England can remember the periodic visits of gypsies to cities and country towns. Here a Romany father leans upon his harp while his two sons demonstrate their skill with rosin-dusted violins. The photograph was made in 1878, apparently from a window of L.V. Newell's studio. Newell's rooms overlooked High Street from the old wooden Peduzzi Building, which was razed in 1890.

Patch Collection

19

19. Gaunt and forlorn in 1923, these massive brick structures seem to look back to their heyday at the turn of the century, when they were regarded as Portsmouth's most notorious saloons and houses of ill fame. On the corner of Water (now Marcy) and State streets stood the Hotel Glocester, Mary Baker, proprietress. The legendary Mrs. Baker is best remembered for her genteel manner and her striking appearance—enhanced by the two diamonds set into her front teeth. The next structure to the left was a saloon kept by Mrs. Anna Dixon, while beyond that was William Dunn's barroom and the "Workman's Social Club."

The character of society changed markedly around the corner, however, and the buildings that lined State Street, to the right of the photograph, were for the most part fine private residences. While later years have seen the destruction of the Water Street saloons, they have simultaneously witnessed the conversion of the brick houses of State Street into stores and restaurants.

Patch Collection

20. *I do not know of any spot with such a fascinating air of dreams and idleness about it as the old wharf . . . . The very fact that it was once a noisy, busy place, crowded with sailors and soldiers—in the war of 1812—gives an enchanting emphasis to the quiet that broods over it today. The lounger who sits of a summer afternoon on a rusty anchor fluke in the shadow of one of the silent warehouses, and looks on the lonely river as it goes murmuring past the town, can not be too grateful to the India trade for having taken itself off elsewhere.*

What a slumberous, delightful, lazy place it is! The sunshine seems to lie a foot deep on the planks of the dusty wharf, which yields up to the warmth a vague perfume of the cargoes of rum, molasses, and spice that used to be piled upon it . . . . I know of many a place where the scenery is more varied and striking; but there is a mandragora quality in the atmosphere here that holds you to the spot, and makes the half hours seem like minutes . . . . I could fancy a man sitting on the end of that old wharf very contentedly for two or three years, provided it could be always June.

Aldrich, *An Old Town By the Sea, 1874*

Near Union Wharf, at the outlet of Puddle Dock, about 1890. The old Sheafe Warehouse, reputed to have been built in 1705, lies behind the dory.

Patch Collection

20

The Maritime Heritage

21 

22 

21. A group of fishing schooners lie at the Ceres Street dock about 1870, drying their sails or carrying on routine repairs. Of Portsmouth's four fish dealers in 1867, three were located on Bow or Ceres Street, near the old Spring Market—the traditional rendezvous of Piscataqua fishermen.

Patch Collection

22. The masts of nine schooners can be discerned in this photograph of the Randall and Caswell fish company on Long Wharf, off Water Street, about 1890. By 1880, the center of commercial fishing in Portsmouth had shifted from its ancient location along Ceres Street to the many deep-water wharves off Water Street, and six fish dealers were in this area by 1886. This photograph, though a double exposure, is significant in showing the many fish "flakes," or drying racks upon which salt cod was cured.

Patch Collection

23. Here, at about the turn of the century, is the death of Long Wharf. One building that survives from John W. Caswell's once-flourishing Portsmouth Fish Company stands staunch and square but hardly accessible at the end of a pier whose planking is rotten and whose pilings seem to have been bent by the north wind. Across the river may be seen the new focus of Portsmouth's maritime energies—the Navy Yard, which was undergoing an extensive modernization even as Long Wharf crumbled away.

Patch Collection

24. As Portsmouth's activity in general shipping and fishing declined, a rapid increase in the amount of coal brought to the port compensated for the loss of other trade. The wharves at the lower end of Market Street became crowded with extensive coal pockets, at which huge steam diggers, like those seen here at the Walker pier, tirelessly unloaded the cargo of the colliers at the rate of several tons a minute. This vast commerce had begun tentatively in 1831, when Edward F. Sise imported thirty-five tons of Lehigh Coal. By 1905, the amount of coal passing through the Boston and Maine Railroad's section of the coal pockets alone was 358,918 tons. Over half a million tons were annually shipped by rail from the several Portsmouth coal pockets to the mills of Manchester and other inland places.

A totally new type of cargo vessel—the multi-masted coal schooner—sustained this booming trade. The first five-masted schooner was built in 1890. The *John B. Prescott,* seen here just after 1900, was launched in 1899 by Holly M. Bean of Camden, Maine, and was probably the third "five-sticker" built. She displaced 2,454 tons net—larger even than the 1,611-ton Portsmouth-built *Typhoon* (the largest clipper ever built in the United States at her launching in 1851). Six-masted colliers were larger still. Though these vessels were exceedingly economical and efficient sailers and represented the last refinement of wooden shipbuilding, they relied on the winds and so gave way at last to steam freighters that could maintain more regular schedules.

Patch Collection

23

24

25 

26 

25. The tidewater towns upriver from Portsmouth had no need of the railroad to supply them with coal; the big schooners were simply towed to their destinations. The 2,193-ton *Paul Palmer,* here seen under tow on the Piscataqua, was the smallest of the five-masters in the fifteen-vessel "Palmer fleet" of white-painted colliers. She was built by George L. Welt at Waldoboro, Maine, in 1902 and ended her days in 1913 when she burned to the water-line north of Race Point, Cape Cod. William F. Palmer, manager of the fleet, once boasted that "we build them with about three times as much timber as they should have to provide for their decay, knowing that there may come a time when one rib in three will have to furnish the strength . . . ." Most of the big colliers were known for their suppleness rather than their rigidity, however. Captain Charles A. Drew of the Portsmouth tug *Piscataqua* summed up the opinion of his colleagues when he joked that the huge schooners were "built of hoop poles and caulked with eel-grass—limber as a snake."

Patch Collection

26. Wrecks were frequent and often fatal along the treacherous New Hampshire coast. The violent gale of Sunday, November 27, 1898, wrought havoc upon shipping in the area. The little two-masted schooner *Iva Bell,* hailing from Belfast, Maine, went ashore at Odiorne's Point early in the morning—the first wreck of the day to be reported. The patrol from the Jerry's Point life saving station managed to

27

28

save the schooner's crew by breeches buoy, and sent an alert to Portsmouth for a tugboat to try to get a line to the vessel and haul her off the rocks. The tug *Piscataqua* went out in the afternoon and returned after dark, her salvage attempts useless in the face of waves that were fast breaking the schooner on the ledges.

Patch Collection

27. The elaborate ornamentation of the Jenness Beach Life Saving Station in Rye belies the serious purpose for which the structure was erected in 1874. The building followed a standardized plan developed for all government life-saving stations at the period. Its intricately braced and bracketed design, the epitome of the "Queen Anne" or "stick" style, was actually functional as well as attractive, for the strong trusses that supported the roof overhang and the sturdy buttresses along the sides securely resisted the buffeting of coastal gales. The government architect displayed a symbolic bent as well as an ornamental genius: the hammer-beam trusses on the gable ends are decorated with stylized dolphins, while the rafter-ends at the roof-peak become sea-birds' heads.

Rye was chosen as the site for New Hampshire's first life-saving station with good reason. Between 1764 and 1873, when the station was established at Jenness Beach, the rugged coast off Rye had seen at least twenty-four wrecks, claiming nineteen or more lives.

Patch Collection

28. The crew of the Jenness Beach Life Saving Station pose with the beach cart they hauled to wreck sites. Such carts contained all the implements needed to get a breeches buoy to a foundering vessel, including the Lyle gun which could fire a line hundreds of feet. Life-saving stations were also equipped with one or more surf boats for rescuing stranded mariners.

Patch Collection

29. Portsmouth Harbor received its first lighthouse, a seventy-eight foot wood structure, in 1771 at the insistence of New Hampshire's last royal governor, John Wentworth. This tower survived the Revolution, and was turned over to federal administration in 1791. By 1803, however, the pre-Revolutionary light had deteriorated to the point where replacement was necessary. Joseph Whipple, collector of customs at Portsmouth and a native of the town, was placed in charge of the arrangements. A contract for the frame of the new building was awarded to Benjamin Clark Gilman, "a native of Exeter, some fifteen miles from here . . . of remarkable mechanical ability," as Whipple described him. Gilman has since become known for the fine clocks and mathematical instruments he invented.

Gilman's octagonal tower, seen here, was eighty-five feet high and rested on a stone foundation. It was equipped with a fixed light having eleven lamps and reflectors, which, except for a brief period during the War of 1812, burned steadily until after the Civil War. In 1851, an investigating board had found the light in good structural condition, but they noted that the lamps and spherical reflectors were "old and much worn," with the interior of the lantern "very dirty." Nevertheless, the wooden tower lasted another twenty-six years, finally being replaced by the present iron lighthouse, 1,000 feet to the east, in 1877.

Patch Collection

29

30

31

30. A placid Piscataqua slips quietly past an equally quiescent Navy Yard in 1883. At this time, the burst of activity created by the Civil War had subsided, leaving the yard with only a skeleton crew to maintain its buildings. Not a single new vessel was built here during the eighties, and in this photograph the major activity seems to be the unloading of the four four-masted schooners along the waterfront. The scene would not change markedly until the Spanish-American War, when a vast modernization program was begun.

From left to right: an early timber shed converted as a shipfitters' and shipwrights' shop; the 1852 floating dry dock, evidently with a brigantine under repair; the 1821 general-store building (behind the first schooner), the first brick structure erected at the yard; the 1858 Main Office; the early Santee Shiphouse (behind the second schooner); the lifting shears (behind the bow of the third schooner); and, at the right, the as-yet-undeveloped Seavey's Island, purchased for future expansion in 1866 at a cost of $105,000.

Staples-Herald Collection

31. Belonging to a departed race of giants, two of the great Navy Yard shiphouses dominate its southern waterfront in this picture from the late eighties or early nineties. These vast structures, constructed to shelter the building of ships, were among the oldest yard components to survive until modern times. They were removed shortly before 1900 to provide room for a new power plant.

The building at the left, behind the big lifting shears, was popularly known as the Santee Shiphouse, and was built in 1819. It took its name from that of a forty-four-gun frigate launched from it in 1820. The central building, known as the Alabama Shiphouse, was built about 1814 to house the eighty-six-gun warship *Washington.* In 1817 the building was lengthened and the keel of the seventy-four-gun *Alabama* was laid down on its ways. Extensive delays prevented the completion of the *Alabama* until 1825, and she was kept on the stocks until needed during the Civil War. Re-named the *New Hampshire,* she was launched in 1864 as a stores and depot ship.

The building at the right, built of hammered granite about 1825, was a mast and spar shed. Tied up in front of this building is the U.S.S. *Essex,* built at the Navy Yard in 1874. In the foreground, at a pier on Seavey's Island, is the two-masted schooner *Carrie E. Pickering* of Deer Isle.

Staples-Herald Collection

32. The Franklin Shiphouse, one of the largest in the United States, was completed in 1838. It derived its name from the fact that the U.S.S. *Franklin* was built within it during the decade from 1854 to 1864. As originally built, the shiphouse was 240 feet long, 131 feet wide, and 72 feet from floor to ridge. Its roof was covered with 130 tons of slate. This vast structure was subsequently enlarged and many more vessels, including a number of submarines in the years following 1914, were built within it. Fire destroyed the building on March 10, 1936.

Staples-Herald Collection

33. Seen from the river in 1922, the Franklin Shiphouse exhibits huge doors which were swung back on their ponderous strap hinges for a major launching.

Staples-Herald Collection

34. The massive frame of the Franklin Shiphouse was intricately braced in three directions, and provided several working levels on both sides of the building ways. As recorded in this photograph, repairs were carried out on the ways in 1921 to expedite submarine construction and launching.

Staples-Herald Collection

32

33

34

35. After a decade of construction, the largest wooden ship ever built at the Navy Yard, the U.S.S. *Franklin,* finally leaves the ways on September 17, 1864. This rare photograph probably was taken from Samuel Badger's shipyard in Kittery. The ponderous doors at both ends of the Franklin Shiphouse have been opened to their fullest extent and the shores and river are crowded with onlookers. The mighty *Franklin,* a great steam-screw frigate 265 feet long and displacing 5,170 tons, was acclaimed during its prolonged construction as "the largest war steamer in the world." Despite this statement, and despite the fact that the *Franklin* became Admiral Farragut's flagship in 1867, she was obsolete at her launching in comparison with the iron-clads and the screw sloops that would soon dominate the seas.

The construction of the *Franklin,* like that of the *Constellation* and the *Marion,* was achieved through an administrative fiction in which repair funds, intended for older vessels, were used to construct entirely new ships that were still listed under the old names. Thus the 1864 *Franklin* was theoretically a rebuilding of the old 1815 *Franklin,* a 2,243-ton, seventy-four-gun ship-of-the-line built in Philadelphia. Because maintenance funds for the old ship were limited, construction of the newer vessel had dragged on through the decade from 1854 to 1864.

Staples-Herald Collection

35

36

37

36. The huge bulk of the Alabama Shiphouse, built about 1814, dwarfs the men who work at its rear door and on the roof. Rainwater was collected from the vast roof by a series of conductors, visible on the left, which fed into a large trough about twenty feet from the ground.

Patch Collection

37. Stripped of her proud and warlike accoutrements, the once-mighty frigate U.S.S. *Constitution* lies ignominiously alongside a quay at the Navy Yard, as a group of Masonic visitors pose on her upper catwalk. Few people realize the trials through which Old Ironsides passed before her final restoration in 1927-30. We know Oliver Wendell Holmes' bitter admonition—"Aye, tear her tattered ensign down"—and the public sentiment that his 1830 poem aroused for the preservation of the old warship. Many assume that the *Constitution* was restored to her original grandeur at that time, and maintained thereafter. She was, in fact, repaired several times during the nineteenth century. But in 1882, she arrived in tow at Portsmouth and was housed over as seen here. She was used for a time as a receiving ship and then as a museum, and became a popular attraction despite her undignified condition. In 1891, for example, the local Storer Post of the G.A.R. held a "reception and colonial party" on board. When the hundredth anniversary of the frigate's 1797 launching approached, the Secretary of the Navy ordered her back to her birthplace, and she arrived at the Boston Navy Yard on September 21, 1897.

Patch Collection

38. The legendary frigate is repaired and retired from combat service. After a long and splendid career as a fighting vessel, the *Constitution* was hauled out for extensive renovation at Portsmouth in 1857. She is seen in this photograph almost completely rebuilt and ready for launching as a training ship.

38

39

The difficult feat of rebuilding the 2,200-ton frigate was accomplished through the use of the Portsmouth Navy Yard's then-new floating dry dock and marine railway. The dry dock and its machinery, completed in 1852 at the fantastic cost of $1,282,000, were denounced as a corrupt waste of money and as an assured failure. Nevertheless, the installation proved its value in hauling out the old 2,243-ton, seventy-four-gun *Franklin* before that vessel was broken up, and was eminently successful in lifting the *Constitution* for repairs. A contemporary description of the dry dock explains this scene well: "At the head of the dock basin [with its floating dock] is a railway, on an inclination of one inch in ten feet, on which the ships may be drawn by an hydraulic machine, operated by steam. The ship, after being drawn upon this railway, is securely shored on a stone foundation laid for this purpose." The steam boiler and hydraulic winch may be seen to the left, and the interior of the wooden floating dock to the right of this classic photograph. Shortly after the picture was made, the *Constitution* was gently placed back in the water by the sophisticated apparatus.

Staples-Herald Collection

39. Work on the temporary housing proceeds after the *Constitution*'s return to the Navy Yard in 1882. The ship is docked under the big shear legs—a location that was to become her traditional berth during the fifteen years that she spent at Portsmouth. These immense shears, capable of lifting 100 tons, were used for stepping masts and installing boilers and heavy machinery in vessels. Shortly after this photograph was made, three light masts for a fore-and-aft rig were placed in the *Constitution* in lieu of her heavy ship's masts.

Staples-Herald Collection

U. S. S. CONSTITUTION

41

42

40. Upper deck of the housed-over *Constitution,* looking forward. At this time, the ship served as a museum.

Staples-Herald Collection

41. "Our Ship was a beautiful specimen of Yankee Architecture, and when we lay in dock, was pronounced by all who saw her as a beautiful model." So wrote Joseph T. Downey, a seaman on board the U.S.S. *Portsmouth* just before her record-breaking maiden voyage from Norfolk to the Sandwich Islands. Built at the Portsmouth Navy Yard in 1843, the vessel was one of the last Navy ships constructed without steam power, and provided a worthy culmination of the age of sail. Designed by Josiah Barker, the master shipbuilder of the Portsmouth yard, the *Portsmouth* was a twenty-four-gun first-class ship sloop of 1,022 tons, and continued in service as a training ship for the New Jersey Naval Militia until 1911. Her keel was laid down on June 15, 1843, and she was launched on October 23 of the same year, though she was not ready to commission for over a year.

Just after her launching, the *Portsmouth* sailed to California, where she was instrumental in its conquest. Parties from the ship raised the first American flags at Sonoma and Yerba Buena (later San Francisco) on July 9, 1846. Later, the *Portsmouth* pursued a varied career which included duty off the coast of Africa in subduing the slave trade and trips to China as well as to the east and west coasts of South America.

This photograph, probably dating from the 1870s, shows the *Portsmouth* at her home port, with the old floating dry dock in the background. Sails, frocks, and jackets are strung up to dry in the breeze.

Patch Collection

42. The steam-and-sail gunboat U.S.S. *Alliance,* her smoothbore nine-inchers projecting below the lifeboats, lies alongside a hoisting scow at the Navy Yard in the late nineteenth century. Launched in 1875 as the *Huron* at the Norfolk Navy Yard, the *Alliance* saw varied duty including service in the North and South Atlantic, Europe and Asia. She was a training ship from 1895 until 1903.

The scene epitomizes the light fitting-out of a vessel in the days before complete mechanization. Power for the derrick in the foreground seems to have been supplied by capstans mounted at the stern of the barge. A span of oxen—universally esteemed in shipyards for their strength, steadiness, and versatility—stand patiently with their teamster near the ship.

Staples-Herald Collection

43. The gunboat U.S.S. *Galena*, a group of tars perched jauntily on her bowsprit, rests at the Portsmouth Navy Yard, probably in 1885 or 1886.

Built at Norfolk in 1879, she was largely employed in Caribbean service protecting American "interests." In 1881 the *Galena* also engaged in relief missions in the Aegean Sea after a severe earthquake at Kastro, Chios. At that time her steam launch (seen alongside her in this photograph) was used to ferry relief supplies to the sufferers.

The *Galena* and her tug went aground off Martha's Vineyard as she was being towed to Portsmouth in 1891 to be fitted with new boilers. Though she was later salvaged, she was finally sold by the Navy in 1892.

Staples-Herald Collection

44. A guard of United States Marines lines the deck of the U.S.S. *Galena* at Portsmouth in 1883.

Staples-Herald Collection

45. Well scrubbed and painted, the U.S.S. *Constellation* lies at a quay in the Portsmouth Navy Yard in 1884. Built at Norfolk in 1853-55 as the Navy's last sailing man-of-war, she put in at Portsmouth during the eighties where she served as a school ship.

Patch Collection

43

44

46. Looking slightly unconvinced that any real opposition is in the offing, a group of cadets practices "Repelling Boarders" drill with muskets and cutlasses on board the U.S.S. *Constellation* in the 1880s.

Patch Collection

45

46

47

48

49

50

47. The U.S.S. *Marion*, seen here adjacent to the old floating dry dock at the Navy Yard, was built at Portsmouth between 1871 and 1873. She was a ten-gun steam sloop of 1,900 tons, and remained on the east coast between 1876, when she was commissioned, and 1885. Thereafter, the *Marion* served in the Pacific, finally becoming a training ship for the California State Naval Militia until her sale in 1907.

This photograph, probably taken by L.V. Newell, reveals that a careful photographer could lavish almost as much attention on a "mundane" subject like a ship as on a portrait. Considerable retouching was employed on the glass plate to improve the picture. The ship's water line has been emphasized by scratching through the emulsion with a needle and by applying ink to the negative to whiten the water. Similarly, the faintly-defined rigging of the ship has been overscored with a razor to give it proper contrast. Even the men at work aloft have been silhouetted more strongly by careful work with a needle. The end result is a crisp ship's portrait instead of the insipid picture that was potentially on the unretouched negative.

Patch Collection

48. Smiling sailors gather for the photographer in the waist of the U.S.S. *Marion.*

Patch Collection

49. A group of Navy Yard workmen, dressed for the winter, pause amid their repairs of the U.S.S. *Marion* at the Navy Yard. After her original construction, the *Marion* returned to Portsmouth in the winter of 1882, and departed for the Pacific in 1885. This must have been the period during which this photograph was made.

Some men in this picturesque group of craftsmen can be identified:

William Hammond, top left, ship carpenter; George Hayes, top right, machinist; James (?) Lydston, center, long beard, carpenter(?); Mark Fernald, center, side whiskers, rigger; William H. Anderson, right, watch cap; Herbert Billings, possibly in center, with screwdriver.

Patch Collection

50. Ten old salts strike a formal pose on board the U.S.S. *Hartford* in 1877. The *Hartford*, a first-class screw sloop-of-war, was Admiral Farragut's flagship at New Orleans, Vicksburg, Port Hudson, and Mobile Bay.

Staples-Herald Collection

51

52

51. The *Benicia*, a 2,400-ton steam screw sloop, lies alongside a quay at the Navy Yard with the city of Portsmouth for a backdrop. Launched at Portsmouth in 1868 as the *Algoma*, the ship was renamed before being commissioned in December, 1869. The *Benicia* served most of her duty in the Pacific, taking part in Rear Admiral John Rodgers' expedition to Korea in 1871 and enjoying the distinction of having transported King Kalakana of Hawaii to San Francisco in 1874.

Patch Collection

52. The famous words of Admiral Dewey at the battle of Manila Bay—"You may fire when ready, Gridley"—brought action not only from Captain Gridley of the U.S.S. *Olympia*, but, more significantly, from S.J. Skaw, the gunner at one of the ship's forward turrets. As one account melodramatically put it, "at nineteen minutes of six o'clock, at a distance of 5,500 yards, the starboard 8-inch gun in the forward turret roared forth a compliment to the Spanish Forts." In a more quiet moment, when the *Olympia* was docked at Portsmouth, photographer L.V. Newell immortalized the proud gunner at his weapon.

Staples-Herald Collection

53. The vast interior of the Franklin Shiphouse dwarfs the U.S.S. *Boxer*, one of the last sailing vessels built in it. The little 346-ton training brigantine was launched in 1904. Here the *Boxer* is seen at her completion, with a launching platform at the bow. The view is toward the landward end of the shiphouse, the big launching doors being at the opposite end.

Patch Collection

54. The year 1899 saw the commence-

53

54

ment of one of the most monumental engineering tasks ever undertaken at the Portsmouth Navy Yard—construction of the vast granite Dry Dock No. 2 in the natural depression between Dennett's and Seavey's Islands. The job, which finally cost $1,070,000, was undertaken by granite contractor John Pierce of New York City, a native of Maine with access to every large quarry in that state. Civil engineer Lee Treadwell superintended the work. Treadwell needed all his prior experience in building "subaqueous foundations" to hold back the tidewater at both ends of the excavation.

The channel between the two islands, formerly known as "Jenkins' Gut," proved to have a solid rock bed. A total of 166,000 cubic yards of rock were blasted away using steam drills and dynamite. This photograph, dating from 1901, shows the drills at work at the far end of the excavation and the large temporary traveling bridge cranes used during construction. After the site was excavated, some 18,000 cubic yards of Portland cement concrete were poured as a base for the granite. The floor and walls of the basin were composed of 20,500 cubic yards of granite supplied from quarries on Cape Ann, Massachusetts, and at Mount Desert, Fox Island, Sprucehead, Biddeford, and Frankfort in Maine. About half of the granite was brought to Portsmouth in a rough state and cut to final shape by New England workmen employed on the job. Late in 1903, after most of the stone had been laid, a cofferdam broke and the inrush of waters threw down the derricks, engines, and boilers. The equipment was quickly restored to order and the 750-foot dock was completed as one of the world's largest and finest.

Patch Collection

55

56

55. When it was finally completed in 1904, the Portsmouth dry dock was 750 feet long, 130 feet wide, and 39 feet from the coping to the floor.

In this photograph, taken in the late 1920s, the dock contains two vessels: the 4,000-ton V-4, representing one of the largest types of American submersibles built before recent advances and, by contrast, a miniature submarine. The gable-roofed building at the right, with a dormer and windows in the roof, is the granite spar shed that once stood with the Santee and Alabama shiphouses, and represents the old southern boundary of the original shipyard.

Staples-Herald Collection

56. In 1907, after the stone dry dock had been officially accepted, the old floating dry dock of 1852 was towed away by the tugs *Mitchell Davis, Portsmouth,* and *Piscataqua* and burned at Revere Beach, Massachusetts, on June 22.

Patch Collection

57. An unlikely occupant of the building ways, a blimp lies in the Franklin Shiphouse in 1915. The airship was put together in the yard's mold loft by a German contracting firm, and was then taken to the shiphouse to be inflated.

Patch Collection

57

58

58. Not all the fine ships built in the lower Piscataqua River were the products of the Navy Yard. Badger's Island and mainland Kittery saw the completion of many a splendid and legendary vessel. And on the Portsmouth side of the river scores of outstanding ships, from the 50-gun *America* of 1749 to the record-breaking clippers of George Raynes and his rivals in the 1850s and later, emerged from civilian shipyards.

The end of a part of this proud tradition was recorded by the photographer on August 5, 1886, as the *Lizzie J. Call* was prepared for launching at Freeman's Point. This three-masted schooner, displacing 195 tons, was the last sizeable sailing vessel ever launched in Portsmouth. Her builder, William Fernald, had outlasted his post-Civil War competitors Daniel Marcy, Prior and Plummer, and Tobey and Littlefield to have the sad distinction of closing an era of Portsmouth's history that had begun in the seventeenth century.

Patch Collection

59

59. A shocking contrast to the pastoral scene of the launching of the *Lizzie J. Call* from Freeman's Point in 1886 is this view of the launch of the 8,800-ton *Babboosic* from the same site thirty-three years later. The beautiful Freeman's Point had undergone vast changes since the halcyon days when it was used for agriculture and light shipbuilding. In 1900 the White Mountain Paper Company bought the site and erected one of the world's largest paper factories there, with buildings covering twenty-two acres. Despite its magnitude, this operation failed within a few years.

In January, 1918, the Atlantic Corporation was founded, and contracted with the Emergency Fleet Corporation to build ten steel vessels of 8,800 tons each. After purchasing the plant and holdings of the White Mountain Paper Company, the Atlantic Corporation swiftly converted the buildings into a modern shipyard, and simultaneously constructed Atlantic Heights, a self-contained village adjacent to the shipbuilding plant, to house the employees. The first keel was laid on May 23, 1918, and the ship, the *Kisnop,* was launched on January 18, 1919—a record completion time for a new shipyard. The *Babboosic,* identical to the *Kisnop,* followed soon after.

Patch Collection

Commercial Town; Industrial City

60

60. This photograph of the Athenaeum in 1900 provides some hint of the dignity that invested Portsmouth's commerce in an earlier day. The building, completed in 1805 as the office of the New Hampshire Fire and Marine Insurance Company, was one of the mercantile focal points of the town. The finest workmen of the area were employed on the structure. The architect of this impressive building, and probably of the structures that flank it, was Bradbury Johnson (1766-1820), who was born in Epping, New Hampshire, and who had helped to design and build some of the finest edifices in nearby Exeter. The joiner's work was done by James Nutter (1775-1855), who was "the head of his craft" in Portsmouth and, as his design for the Portsmouth Academy (now the Public Library) proves, was a skilled architect in his own right. The carved ornaments of the facade of the office building are the work of William Dearing (1759-1813), a noted ship and architectural carver.

The Nelson-Harris building to the left of the Athenaeum once housed the Portsmouth Bank, founded in 1803 to manage the finances of the adjacent insurance company. A curved cornice, identical to the one that sweeps upward from the building on the right, once linked the two buildings.

Patch Collection

61. One of the most significant commercial structures in Portsmouth is the New Hampshire Bank building on Market Square, here seen in its original condition in an 1877 photograph. This structure, built after the devastating fire of 1802, housed New Hampshire's first bank (founded in 1792), and is said to be the earliest building in the United States built and continuously used for banking purposes. Notable lawyers, including Jeremiah Mason, Levi Woodbury, and Franklin Pierce, have occupied its upper floors.

The design of the unusual U-shaped building has been attributed to the merchant Eliphalet Ladd, who was

61

62

involved in the bank's affairs. In 1882, the facade was somewhat altered with a symmetrical Victorian front, and in 1904, the building underwent a redesigning that totally obscured its early character. The southern half of the building now has a somewhat Italianate facade of granite. The northern side (including the small adjacent space to the north formerly occupied by True Priest's once-popular saloon) is covered with a monumental front that bespeaks the powerful classical influence of the Ecole des Beaux Arts on American designers in the early twentieth century.

Patch Collection

62. Picturesque in its own right and supplanting a still more picturesque predecessor, the fish market (center) on Spring Hill near the intersection of Ceres and Bow streets, still survived as an important local institution when this photograph was made in the 1870s. Probably built during the 1840s, the market building seen here was rented by the city to local fish dealers like Richard L. Randall and John W. Caswell, whose sign may be discerned in the photograph. Randall and Caswell occupied the building as partners from about 1867 until about 1881.

The previous market house at this location—built on nearby Market Street in 1761 and moved to this waterfront site about thirty years later—was of the old open type with free public stalls. There, as Charles W. Brewster fondly recollected, the coarse and colorful housewives of Kittery and Eliot, having arrived in a dozen canoes, were accustomed to jostle with local fishermen for space while crying out in shrill voices the virtues of their produce.

By 1883 even the fish dealers who had supplanted the fishwives moved away. In 1895 Spring Market became a ferry landing owned by the Portsmouth, Kittery and York Street Railway.

Staples-Herald Collection

63. Though granite quarrying and cutting techniques had been perfected in New England in the early nineteenth century (largely through the impetus provided by the construction of the Bunker Hill monument) few stone buildings were ever constructed in Portsmouth. Among those few stone commercial buildings was the "Stone Store" that once stood on lower Market Street, near the end of Russell Street. Granite for the monumental engineering works of the Navy Yard and for the Stone (Unitarian) Church in Portsmouth was brought by water from Rockport, Mass., and Maine quarries, and the expense of cutting and transporting it may have precluded its widespread use in Portsmouth.

This photograph, made between 1895 and 1905, shows the Stone Store in company with the shops, firewood storage sheds and coal buildings that once occupied Market Street. The stone building, which was probably constructed in the 1830s, was occupied as early as 1860 by Joshua Brooks, a grain and flour merchant. By 1871, Brooks was in partnership with Henry A. Yeaton, whose name may be read on the facade, and from the 1880s the firm operated a steam grist mill and a grain elevator on Bridge Street. The mill operated until 1918 and was the last survivor of an industry that had begun with the construction of John Pickering's grist mill at the South Mill Dam in 1658.

Patch Collection

64. One of Portsmouth's most unusual commercial structures was the "stone stable" on Fleet Street, here recorded shortly before its demolition in 1905. The building was constructed in 1836, as the dated stone in its gable end attests. It was probably built as an adjunct to the adjacent "Temperance Mansion House" hotel, the converted mid-eighteenth century dwelling of Dr.

Ammi R. Cutter which re-opened in 1836 under the management of Joseph E. Robinson. For several decades the hotel and its stable continued to operate under various names, including the "City Hotel" and the "National Hotel." When the hotel burned in 1877 and was replaced by Frank Jones' "National Block" (seen at the left), the stone building assumed an independent life of its own as one of Portsmouth's largest livery stables.

Patch Collection

65

66

65. Seen in a photograph of about 1900, Henry C. Hopkins' dry goods store stands in splendor above its less embellished Market Street neighbors. Thomas Bailey Aldrich had noted in 1874, "Market Street is the stronghold of the dry-goods shops," and the statement was equally true at the turn of the century. It is the epitome of the formal and ostentatious business establishment of the Edwardian era. The massive eagle under the cornice of the building is the work of John Haley Bellamy (1836-1914), the noted carver of Kittery and Portsmouth.

Patch Collection

66. This photograph, made between 1881 and 1883, is a rare visual record of a forgotten New England phenomenon, the rural basketmaker. Several towns near Portsmouth sustained enclaves of such individuals, who lived more like gypsies than Yankees and were generally distrusted by their more conventional neighbors. One such group occupied the tract contemptuously dubbed "Leathers City" in Barrington. Another clan, pictured here, were the "hill people of Sasanoa," who lived at the base of Mount Agamenticus in York, Maine.

Patch Collection

67

68

67. Twentieth century mobility, which brings every potential customer to a store to suit his needs, offers only a dubious advancement from the older system that brought the purveyor to the customer's doorstep. Whether the housewife needed ice, coal, meat, milk, groceries, bakery products, kerosene, tinware, or the limitless bounty of the mail-order catalogue, the products were once hand-delivered. The merchants who first understood the appeal of this system became legends in their own time. Such a man was Charles David Garland, of West Rye, whose Yankee enterprise in shipping 15,000 bushels of potatoes and 300 tons of hay in a single year won him a place in the town's published history. Garland opened his general store in 1879 when he was thirty, and continued in business until the 1920s. He made himself almost indispensable to his neighbors when he became the West Rye postmaster in 1885 and a justice of the peace.

Garland's grocery wagon, probably with the owner himself at the reins, is seen here at about the turn of the century. In the background is the store and "photograph rooms" of Alba R.H. Foss, at the shore end of Washington Road in Rye.

Patch Collection

68. "Rapid delivery" must have been the motto of this milkman, whose Buick truck, painted an antiseptic white, obviously boasted neither refrigeration nor much carrying capacity.

Patch Collection

69

69. A bewildering but encouraging array of remedies greeted the visitor to Benjamin Green's newly-opened drug store on Market Square in 1899. Only the expert knowledge of the proprietor, who had worked his way up from clerk to owner in a neighboring store, could have retrieved a specific item from the hundreds of nostrums that filled the shelves, cabinets and showcases.

The decor of the 1805 building had been thoroughly modernized to accommodate the new business. The shop was illuminated by fixtures that combined gas and electricity. The ceiling of pressed tin displayed a rococo design of airy lightness, as did the cornices of the wall cabinets. The young proprietor, seen behind the counter, had good reason to take pride in this stylish pharmacopoeia, over which he was destined to preside until his retirement four decades later.

Patch Collection

70

70. Photographed in June, 1900, the coal office of Gray and Prime, successors to the mercantile concern of E.F. Sise and Company, displays clear evidence of the firm's historic dependence on the sea. The original organization, founded by Edward Fleetford Sise in 1818, had been concerned with general shipping, and specialized in the importation and sale of "Crockery and Glass ware." The emphasis of the business began to shift in 1831, however, when Sise's packet schooner *Fawn* arrived in port with thirty-five tons of Lehigh lump coal from Philadelphia—the first "sea coal" ever brought to Portsmouth. Thereafter, coal importation gradually became the principal business of the firm, and coal's increasing importance to New Hampshire's railroads and industries stimulated the establishment of competing companies. By 1915, Portsmouth was the coal port for all of New Hampshire and much of Maine and Vermont. In 1896, the Sise firm was purchased by two former clerks in the office, Charles W. Gray and Herbert O. Prime, who specialized in Wilkes-Barre coal and Worcester salt and who employed fifteen to thirty workmen with six to twelve teams in constant service.

This photograph portrays an almost forgotten aspect of American business. At the left, behind the disconnected coal stove, is a gas-lighted clerk's desk. Within the barrier may be seen a letter-press, two roll-top desks lighted by gas, and a mineral cabinet displaying the specialties of the firm. The half-hull lift models of Piscataqua vessels comprise one of the finest single collections ever assembled, and largely represent

71

72

ships built by George Raynes and Tobey and Littlefield.

Patch Collection

71. A group of office workers, teamsters, and coal shovelers pose beside the coal bunkers and woodsheds of J. Albert Walker's Portsmouth Coal Pockets at the turn of the century. The Walker firm employed from forty to a hundred people, most of them laborers. Anthracite coal retailed for about six dollars a ton, while kindling wood sold for two or three cents a bundle at this period. Cordwood, like that stacked in the background, was also sold by the firm, and still provided the source of heat for many an old-fashioned Portsmouth house.

Patch Collection

72. From 1658 until 1881, the impounded tidewater of the South Mill Pond turned the wheels or turbines of industry at the venerable mill dam. Here, during the 1870s, the photographer has captured the last days of commercial activity at the site. A few years later, the city purchased the water privilege and removed the old mill structure at the left, ending one of the longest-lived tidemill operations in New England.

For many years after 1658, when John Pickering was granted the privilege of constructing a mill here, the waterpower at this site seems to have been used exclusively for gristmilling. Fresh water streams upriver, nearer the sources of timber, were harnessed for the sawmills that had proliferated by the end of the 1600s and had transformed the Piscataqua region into one of the most heavily industrialized areas in seventeenth-century North America. By the mid-nineteenth century, however, machinery for planing architectural mouldings from wood had been perfected and made it desirable to establish woodworking mills close to town. Accordingly, the South Mill not only served as one of Portsmouth's two grist mills by the 1860s, but was also operating as a sawing and planing mill under the management of Nathan W. Tarleton.

Staples-Herald Collection

73

74

73. The North Mill, last survivor (it closed about 1888) of the age of water-powered industry in Portsmouth, is silhouetted against the trees of aptly-named Elm Street (now part of Maplewood Avenue) in the late seventies or early eighties. The North Mill Pond, referred to in the seventeenth century as Fresh Creek, was originally the site of one of Portsmouth's first mills, established by John Cutt about 1659. This mill, however, was powered by the fresh-water stream that flows into the head of the pond under Bartlett Street rather than by the surging tidewater of the pond itself. It was not until 1764 that the town granted Peter Livius the privilege of damming the pond's outlet for a tide-mill.

By the mid-nineteenth century, the North Mill, like that at the South Mill Pond, was utilized both for grinding grain and for woodworking.

Staples-Herald Collection

74. From the mid-1830s until about 1895, the Goodrich Tanyard was a landmark on the Christian Shore side of the North Mill Dam. It was the last survivor of this once-flourishing trade. The ancient tannery itself, here shown as it appeared about 1880, may have been built in the late 1700s. During the eighteenth century, the area of the North Mill Pond had become the focus of Portsmouth's tanning industry.

The survival of the Goodrich Tannery may be attributed, in part, to the remarkable energy and longevity of its nineteenth-century owner, Moses Horoe Goodrich. Goodrich was at work here at least as early as 1839, when he was twenty-four, and continued until 1895, when he retired at eighty. With his death at ninety in 1905, the ancient trade of "Tanner and Currier" ceased to exist in Portsmouth.

Staples-Herald Collection

75. A survival from the 1830s, the sailmaking business of John R. Holbrook continued until 1884 in this picturesque gambrel-roofed shop. The old building, which occupied a now-vacant lot on Market Street opposite the Moffatt-Ladd House, also had a lower level which was accessible from Ceres Street and which housed George J. Fernald's boat-building shop after the mid-1870s.

From the late thirties until 1875, when a third shop appeared, Holbrook was one of two sailmakers active in

75

76

Portsmouth. He made not only sails, but also awnings, tents, canvas bags, and other items of duck.

After Holbrook's death, the sail loft served for a number of years as a shoemaker's and a carpenter's shop, each with its own entrance from Market Street. Fernald continued to build boats in the rear of the building until about 1915.

Patch Collection

76. In the intellectual history of New Hampshire, this humble wooden building was a towering monument. Here, in 1756, the printer Daniel Fowle set up the first printing press in New Hampshire, and began to publish the colony's first newspaper. The old building, which was owned by Fowle as late as 1772, is said to have been built specifically as his printing office. It stood at the junction of Washington and Pleasant Streets, immediately south of Howard Street, and its walls conformed to the angle of the street intersections. The building was later used as a dwelling house, and was removed about 1878 to be replaced by the brick John Colcord House that still stands on the site.

Born in Charlestown, Fowle began his printing career in Boston in 1740. In 1754, he was suddenly arrested by order of the Massachusetts House of Representatives "on *suspicion*" of having printed a pamphlet entitled *The Monster of Monsters*, by Tom Thumb, Esq., which reflected upon some of the House members. Although Fowle denied having printed the offending pamphlet, he could not deny that both his brother Zechariah and his black pressman Primus had been involved in its publication. Consequently Fowle was taken to the "common gaol" at ten o'clock in the evening, and closely confined there without visitors "among thieves and murderers." Told that he might go after two days, Fowle steadfastly refused, "observing, that as he was confined at midnight uncondemned by law, he desired that the authority that confined, should liberate him, and not *thrust him out privily.*" Finally taking his liberty because of his wife's ill health, Fowle was so soured by these arbitrary and tyrannical procedures that he accepted an invitation to remove to Portsmouth, where he remained until his death in 1787.

Patch Collection

77

78

77. The ancient Nathaniel Rogers House of 1705, its venerable character thoroughly disguised, ends its days perched atop a row of stores. The old building had begun its existence when the town granted its minister, the Rev. Mr. Rogers, £150 to help him replace his old residence which had been destroyed by fire. Antiquarians have noted that this was "the first house in town in which square panes of glass were used instead of the diamond shaped"—a statement that may imply the use of vertical sliding sash rather than outward-swinging casements. Such sash also first appeared in Boston around 1705.

The building remained in the Rogers family until 1871. Soon thereafter the entire structure was raised about 10 feet to provide shop space for John S. Tilton, harnessmaker and Adolph Robeck, baker. By 1902, the date of this photograph, Robeck had been succeeded by Baldwin A. Reich's "fancy bakery," while Tilton had been supplanted by Charles E. and William F. Woods. The Woods establishment, recognizing the coming extinction of their harness business, also dealt in bicycles and trunks. By 1910, William F. Woods was the last harnessmaker in Portsmouth.

The Rogers Building finally suffered the same fate as had its predecessor, being badly damaged by fire and then demolished.

Patch Collection

78. From an early time in Portsmouth's history, processing animal products had been the province not only of the frugal housewife but of the butcher as well. The butcher was often skilled in rendering animal fats into necessities such as tallow candles and soap. This tradition survived intact in Portsmouth until after 1900. Following the Civil War, Harry J. Freeman first began to work as a butcher. By 1869, however, he had commenced the manufacture of soap, and was also a "dealer in tallow, grease, bones, neat's foot oil, &c." By 1888, Freeman was Portsmouth's last surviving soap manufacturer. His factory, shown here, was located on Islington Street at the corner of Aldrich Road—an area that is hardly as rural in appearance today as when this photograph was made before 1900. Freeman also ran a large livery and teaming business, and obviously was well prepared to make good use of the remains of his unfortunate animals when they finally succumbed to the "heavy teaming" he advertised.

Patch Collection

79

79. This huge complex formed the keystone of one of the largest business empires ever developed in northern New England. The Frank Jones Brewing Company—far too extensive to be recorded in any single photograph—drew upon the superior quality of Portsmouth's water supply and upon the aggressive genius of its owner to become one of the most successful and celebrated brewing houses in North America. If Portsmouth had any claim to national recognition in the late nineteenth century, it was for one thing alone: Frank Jones' Ale.

The sprawling brewery of fifty-one buildings, whose extent is only hinted at here, covered a fifteen-acre tract of land and included such auxiliary facilities as two miles of railroad trackage and two yard locomotives, an electric generating plant, an all-important twenty-well private water supply about three-and-a-half miles distant in Newington, and its own pumping station and standpipe.

The Jones Brewery reached its gigantic proportions from humble beginnings. Beginning in 1861 the company produced only 5,300 barrels of ale. Some forty years later, the annual production exceeded a quarter of a million barrels.

Seen in this photograph, from center to left, are a five-story brew house, with vast cisterns in its cellar and offices in the clock tower; a narrow five-story refrigerating plant; a long, low fermenting house; and a flat-roofed cold-storage building. Behind the main brew house, extending parallel to the railroad tracks, are low malt and grain storage buildings. To the right of the tracks are boiler and engine shops.

Patch Collection

80. Shaded by trees, embellished with finials, weathervanes and turrets, and ennobled by a colossal statue that offered a brimming glass of ale to the thirsty passer-by, the Eldredge Brewery's aesthetic appeal may have stolen customers from the titanic Jones Brewery on the opposite side of Islington Street. The establishment began in 1858 as Fisher and Company and was purchased by Heman Eldredge and his son, Marcellus, in 1870. Its growth, though more modest than Jones', was proportionately similar. The first production of the Fisher Brewery was twenty-eight barrels, while less than twenty-five years later the plant was producing "the celebrated Portsmouth ale" at a rate of 300 barrels a day. The company continued its production until World War I.

The large building with the statue, at left, is the "ice vault" for beer storage; it was supplied by an ice pond created by impounding the waters of the nearby fresh creek. The middle structure, with a single cupola on its roof, was used for malt storage and as a rack room. The elaborate building at right, built about 1890, was a wash house and boiler room.

Patch Collection

80

81

81. The smallest of Portsmouth's three major breweries, the Portsmouth Brewing Company, was also the most centrally located. Its plant, established about 1870, was on Bow Street, diagonally behind St. John's Church.

The company, which closed down at the time of World War I, compensated for its lack of size by offering a wide variety of products. During the 1880s, the firm advertised itself as "Brewers of India, Pale, Stock and Cream Ales, Hop Beer and Old Brown Stout." During the early twentieth century the brewers added an exotic beverage that was evidently intended to appeal to both the German and the Yankee: "Portsburger Lager Beer."

This photograph, made between 1875 and 1885, evidently shows nearly every employee of the firm from owner to teamsters.

Patch Collection

Architecture:
The Public Image

82

82. In 1794, the town of Portsmouth bought a lot of land on Pleasant Street, or the Parade as it was then called, for building a public market house. This plan was not carried out until 1800, when a fine two-story brick building, eighty feet long, was completed. The structure followed the plan common to earlier market buildings like Faneuil Hall in Boston or the Old Brick Market in Newport. Its first story, twelve feet high, had a series of arched openings that provided access to ten merchants' stalls. The second story, fourteen feet high, was a single large auditorium called Jefferson Hall, and was used for town and public meetings. This striking building, which gave Market Square its name, was completed at a cost of slightly over $7,000. Its master joiner, and probably its architect, was Bradbury Johnson of Exeter, who was soon to design the Athenaeum building on the north side of Market Square.

Tragically, the fire of 1802 consumed all but the brick walls of the building. The shell was roofed over in 1803, however, and the interior was fully restored by 1805. Thereafter, the building continued its dual function as market-place and meeting-place for six decades.

In 1864, however, Jefferson Hall was subdivided into "City Rooms," and the Market House became, in effect, the city hall. In 1873, the exterior of the old building was remodelled as seen in this photograph, and in 1875 the market stalls, which had incongruously continued to occupy the same building as the city government, were abolished. Thereafter, the entire structure was used as the city hall until the 1858 high school was converted for the use of the municipal government in 1910.

This photograph reveals the old market house arches along the sides of the building. The structure was replaced by the New Hampshire National Bank (now the Indian Head Bank) about 1912.

Patch Collection

83. The era of Greek Revival architecture was not a period of vigorous building activity in Portsmouth, although the town was favorably disposed toward the style. Local critics as early as 1826 were sufficiently interested in ancient design to object to the belfry on the granite Unitarian Church as a disfigurement that prevented the building from representing "a perfect model of classic architecture." Despite this degree of interest, the town did not see its first example of "pure Grecian" architecture until 1832, when the diminutive Episcopal Chapel was built on State Street.

The building was erected by John Fisher Sheafe from designs selected by the Rev. Dr. Charles Burroughs, rector of St. John's Church. The master builder was William Tucker, one of Portsmouth's leading joiners and contractors during the 1820s and 1830s. As Portsmouth joiners had done since the early eighteenth century, Tucker also executed some of his best joiner's work on locally built vessels.

Shortly after the time of its completion, the Episcopal Chapel became the home of the Brattle Organ, one of the most historically significant musical instruments in America. The organ was

83

brought to Boston by Thomas Brattle in 1713, and was probably the first pipe organ in the colonies. After being used in King's Chapel until 1756, and in St. Paul's Church in Newburyport until 1836, the instrument was purchased for the Portsmouth chapel by Dr. Burroughs. At that time, the organ was put in a new mahogany-veneered case in the then-current Empire style.

Patch Collection

84. The second of Portsmouth's fully-developed Greek Revival buildings was this Court House, built in 1836 on Court Street when the old State House on Market Square was removed. With its two Doric columns *in antis*, its laurel-wreathed frieze, and its flush-boarded walls, this building was Portsmouth's only true public edifice in the classic style.

When it was deemed necessary to remove the decayed 1758 State House, which had served for years as a Court

84

House, several proposals to provide a new judicial building were advanced. Some persons advocated the purchase of the brick church on the corner of Pleasant and Livermore streets (later converted to an apartment house); some suggested the adaptation of the Academy (now the Public Library); and some favored the moving of the 1758 State House to the Alms House lot on Court Street, where the Central Fire Station now stands. The final solution was the construction of this small but well-designed building on the Alms House lot.

In 1891, a new court house on State Street supplanted this building, which then became the headquarters of the New Hampshire National Guard and the Portsmouth City Band. When the Central Fire Station was built in 1919, the Court House was moved to the rear of the site, where it was damaged by fire and subsequently demolished.

Patch Collection

85. Portsmouth's new high school on Daniel Street, built in 1858, was a decided advance over earlier wooden schoolhouses described by Charles Brewster as "better fit for pigs than for children." The large and well-designed edifice was particularly progressive in its program, since it had facilities for the education of boys and girls in the same building (though in segregated areas until 1873). Earlier practices had dictated separate high school buildings for the sexes; the boys had occupied the old brick schoolhouse near the Methodist Church on State Street, and the girls had been assigned the basement of the Court House on Court Street.

When the high school was built, it was expected to provide ample room for a century of growth. Before 1900, however, it had undergone several remodelings and enlargements, and was finally superseded in 1903. After 1910, it was converted to its present use as City Hall. This photograph shows the building in nearly its original condition.

Patch Collection

86. The most magnificent of Portsmouth's early nineteenth-century gathering places was Franklin Hall, built in 1819 on Congress Street by the prosperous cabinetmaker Langley Boardman. The large second floor room, graced on the outside by an impressive arched window, possessed a spring floor to impart a tireless buoyancy to the dancers' feet. The third floor, lighted on the front by windows with complex tracery, was used as a meeting place by Portsmouth's several Masonic lodges, which had grown too numerous to continue in their old room on the second floor of the Athenaeum.

Next door was a four-story brick hotel constructed by Boardman in 1819, known variously as the "Franklin House," "Robinson's Hotel," and "Portsmouth Hotel."

This photograph, made about 1873, is one of very few views ever made of this striking set of buildings. The entire block was consumed by fire on May 8, 1879, and was immediately replaced by the far more massive Franklin Building that still survives.

Patch Collection

87. This rare ambrotype provides the only record of one of Portsmouth's major early hotels, the Piscataqua House. The large building, with its clapboard front, brick end, and curious shed dormers in the roof, stood upon the Pleasant Street site where the 1858 granite Custom House was later built. This early photograph records the last moments of the old building, and must have been made between June, 1857 (when the building was acquired by the federal government and the hotel establishment moved to the adjacent building on the right), and August, 1857 (when the cornerstone of the new Custom House was laid).

This site had been occupied by a hotel as early as 1818. The structure in this photograph, however, appears to date from the 1830s, at which time it was known as the "Farmers' Hotel," a popular place with country people.

Patch Collection

88. Legend states that when Frank Jones arrived in Portsmouth after his first weary trip from Barrington, he partook of a hearty meal at the Rockingham House, a hotel kept in the converted 1785 dwelling of Woodbury Langdon. This meal was to be the beginning of an extraordinary future for the old hotel, for Jones, grown rich, purchased the building in 1870. This photograph shows the structure as he remodeled it at that time. Jones converted the relatively small original building into an imposing edifice of brick and marble, crowning the whole with a stylish mansard roof. With a solicitude for the colonial past that was rare in the Victorian era, he retained the famed octagonal dining room of the Langdon Mansion, one of the earliest surviving American interiors in the Adamesque style.

The hotel was extensively damaged by fire in 1884, and was immediately rebuilt in its present form under the direction of architect Jabez Sears of Boston.

Staples-Herald Collection

85

86

87

88

89

89. Real table cloths, pressed tin walls and ceiling, and the universal overhead fans greeted the customer at Rowe and Voudy's Cafe on Congress Street. Opened about 1914, Rowe and Voudy's supplanted a once-popular institution of an earlier type—a ladies' oyster saloon—in the same building. The cafe operated in its location near the Granite State Fire Insurance Building until 1940.

Patch Collection

90. Photographer Walter Staples recorded the splendor of the Olympia Theatre on Vaughan Street shortly after its opening in 1916. With its proscenium arch of gilded acanthus leaves and an asbestos curtain that appears to have transported Portsmouthians to the very feet of Mount Olympus, the Olympia offered serious competition to the Music Hall on nearby Chestnut Street. Legitimate theatre did not long retain its vigor in the twentieth century, however; by 1929, with the birth of the "talkies," the Olympia became one of three motion picture theatres in Portsmouth. It remained in operation until about 1950.

Staples-Herald Collection

91. During the long period when each New England town made provisions to maintain its own poor on a municipal farm, Portsmouth had always carefully performed this duty. The first almshouse was established in 1711, and local historians have always taken pride in believing that this was the first pauper workhouse in the colonies. This same spirit of solicitude for the poor prevailed in 1834, when the town completed a large almshouse, shown here, on the recently-purchased Thomas Sheafe farm on Myrtle Street. As a contemporary writer noted:

> It is a large and costly brick building, the roof covered with slate and is capable of accommodating 250 persons. Connected with it is a valuable farm of 170 acres, upon which the male inmates of the house who are able, are required to labor . . . . The cost of the whole was about $32,000.

Previously the town almshouse had been located on Court Street, where the Central Fire Station now stands. The old building, erected in 1755, contained a hall used for town meetings and for the collections of the Portsmouth Social Library. Because the town seemed to cherish this close relationship with the occupants of the almshouse, a sizable minority of persons were in favor of building the 1834 structure on the land that later became Langdon Park rather than in the more remote Myrtle Street location. When the latter site was finally selected, however, the town was determined to make the most progressive agricultural use of its farm. In a town meeting of 1836, it was voted to purchase and set out a quantity of white Chinese mulberry trees in order to attempt to follow the then-current New England enthusiasm for silk production!

Patch Collection

Architecture: The Domestic Image

92

93

94

92. Standing in stately grandeur among its neighbors, the ancient Wentworth House at Puddle Dock looks back three centuries to the first development of the neighborhood that surrounds it. The old house was built about 1695 by John Wentworth, later lieutenant-governor of the province. When the house was constructed, the large hereditary tracts of land on both sides of the creek (later known as Puddle Dock) were first being subdivided into house lots. The Wentworth House was among the first generation of structures erected, and was one of only two or three of the late seventeenth century houses near the creek that survived into the twentieth century.

This unusually large dwelling was probably the most pretentious house in the vicinity. The floors on the larger north side of the house were supported by double summer beams with well-executed decorative chamfering, and the large proportions of the building rendered it a giant in its time. At some point in the early eighteenth century, the fireplace walls on both floors of the house were sumptuously enriched by the addition of cornices of classical correctness and of sheathing and paneling decorated with heavy bolection mouldings.

The proud history of the Wentworth House ended in the early twentieth century. In 1924, the dwelling was sold for $3,500 to the local antique dealer Charles Stewart, who removed the building to the edge of the river and sold much of its fine woodwork to the Metropolitan Museum in New York in 1926. Rooms from the building, fabricated from the second-floor woodwork and from parts of the massive pine frame, can be seen today at the Metropolitan and at Winterthur Museum in Delaware.

Patch Collection

93. The left-hand portion of this house, which stood on the northwest corner of Court and Atkinson streets, is said to have been built about 1700 by John Underwood. Its proportions and size were similar to those of the slightly earlier John Wentworth House on the southern shore of Puddle Dock. The doorway, dormers, and window pediments, as well as the large Atkinson Street wing, are later additions.

Portsmouth's early Roman Catholics held some of their first meetings in this dwelling prior to their establishment of any permanent place of worship. The house was retained by Underwood descendants until the twentieth century. It appears to have been removed shortly before 1914.

Patch Collection

94. This early L-shaped house on Washington Street had fallen into disrepair when the photographer recorded it about 1900. Ninety years earlier, however, the local Methodists first organized their society here in 1808. As was long customary with that sect, the Portsmouth Methodists made effective use of traveling preachers and emotion-charged prayer meetings to gain converts. The local joiner James Nutter, himself later a Methodist Episcopal deacon, described the fervor of one such prayer meeting that he probably attended in this house about 1808, at the electrifying moment of his conversion:

> As I was unacquainted with any such meeting I went in amongst the rest, the room being very full in that part of the house where I was. When the minister says, "Let us pray," all knelt down, old and young, all except myself who stood up like a post. And what to do I could not tell, and how I wished I was out of the meeting—but could not go unless I had trampled on the heads of others. But that I might not be much discovered I leaned over the back of the seat as flat down as possible . . . and in this position all at once I see Jesus Christ in the midst of the sky about the size of a man clad in a garment dipped in blood . . . In a few minutes Christ disappeared, and my feelings—who can describe them?

This structure was obviously built in two parts, the portion nearest the camera being the newer. It is possible that the section facing the street, evidently once a central-chimney dwelling, was the "saltbox" house built on this site for soldier, lumber dealer and jurist Capt. John Hill in 1698 by carpenter Edward Skate and by masons Edward Toogood and Samuel Hill. The old house was torn down about 1910.

Patch Collection

95 

96 

95. From about 1730 until 1920, one of the great early mansion houses of the Piscataqua region dominated the middle section of Daniel Street. The George Jaffrey House stood in solitary grandeur at the crest of a low hill north of Daniel Street, and was connected to the main thoroughfare by its own linden-lined avenue. The house site, the avenue (later named Linden Street), and the very hill itself were obliterated during the construction of the 1967 Federal Office Building. Because the spacious front and rear yards of the Jaffrey House were subdivided and filled with houses and other buildings at the mid-nineteenth century, and because the mansion itself was suffered to deteriorate later in that century, the building was never photographed to advantage.

The Jaffrey Mansion was reminiscent of the great "prodigy houses" of the Elizabethan age—massive, U-shaped in plan, and yet coherent and grand in visual effect. Its many rooms were richly paneled, and several of its fireplaces were framed with imported Delft tiles. On the exterior, its walls were covered with unusual beaded clapboards, and one can suppose that its original front doorway, which had fluted pilasters and Corinthian capitals, was surmounted by a segmental pediment similar to the one on the central dormer.

Staples-Herald Collection

96. A *tour-de-force* of carver's and joiner's work, the Jaffrey Mansion corner cupboard or "beaufait" was one of the finest in New England. This magnificent feature, though probably later than the original woodwork of the house, provided a focal point that was in keeping with the grandeur of the spacious rooms. It may now be seen at the Boston Museum of Fine Arts.

Patch Collection

97

97. From the 1740s through the 1760s, the gambrel-roofed house was a particularly popular style in Portsmouth. One of the finest of this type was built on Vaughan Street about 1760 for George Meserve, soon to be granted (and quickly to renounce) the title of stamp master for the Province of New Hampshire. The structure was one of several attributed to the skilled hand of Michael Whidden III (1733-1818), Portsmouth's finest joiner during the decades immediately preceding and following the Revolution. The Meserve House was one of the great mansions of its period, possessing a splendidly-balustraded stairway lighted by a large arched window, rooms in which all four walls were enriched from floor to ceiling with green-painted paneling, and fireplaces embellished with Delft tiles. In the garden were two mighty sassafras trees (one of which is seen here) of remarkable age and size for that species, and a venerable bergamot pear tree that survived until the mid-nineteenth century.

The house passed into the hands of Meserve's son-in-law, James Sheafe, whose family retained ownership until 1839. Sheafe's tenants included the legendary jurists Jeremiah Mason, who lived here from 1800 to 1808, and Daniel Webster, who made this his first Portsmouth residence.

The house suffered numerous changes in the twentieth century. Most of its fine woodwork was removed, its first floor was altered for stores and restaurants, and a large commercial addition obliterated the old garden on the right. The house was finally removed in 1970 during an urban renewal program.

Patch Collection

98 

99 

98. This magnificently-proportioned gambrel-roofed dwelling was built about 1749 by the Rev. Dr. Samuel Langdon, who had become North Church minister two years previously. Langdon made this building his home until 1774, when he left Portsmouth, perhaps ill-advisedly, to assume the presidency of Harvard College at one of the most difficult periods of its history. After a stormy career at Harvard, Langdon resigned in 1780 to assume ministerial duties at Hampton Falls, where he died in 1797. Until the twentieth century, however, this venerable Pleasant Street house remained in the possession of Langdon descendants.

According to the reminiscences of nonagenarian Capt. Daniel Fernald, as recorded by Charles Brewster in 1859, the Langdon House was "built by Hopestill March of Dover, a mulatto." The somewhat enigmatic March was almost certainly identical with Hopestill Cheswill, who spent much of his life as a housewright in Newmarket, and who is also credited with the construction of the long-destroyed Bell Tavern on Congress Street.

The dwelling was dismantled and re-erected at Old Sturbridge Village, Massachusetts. Its site is now a parking lot. The house seen on the right, the 1794 North Church Parsonage, fortunately survives to give some hint of the former beauty of Pleasant Street.

Patch Collection

99. In 1777, a group of Portsmouth residents, espousing the revolutionary theological doctrine that a loving and fatherly God promised salvation to all men, organized themselves into the Universalist Church. Four years earlier, the group had been inspired by the visit of the English "Apostle of Universalism," John Murray, who left Portsmouth to continue his missionary work elsewhere before settling in nearby Gloucester, Massachusetts. Seeking among their own number for a replacement, the Portsmouth Universalists selected Noah Parker, a blacksmith and tinsmith, to be their unordained minister. The prejudice which soon arose against this liberal sect, with its sometimes-unlettered clergy, is aptly shown in a still-remembered objection voiced by New Hampshire country people in 1788 that the new Federal Constitution did not exclude from office "Turks, Papists, or worst of all, Universalists." New England, with its stern Calvinist convictions of predestinarianism, was hardly prepared for the cheerful promise of universal salvation.

At about the same time that he assumed his ministerial duties, Parker moved from his earlier house at the intersection of Daniel and Penhallow Streets to this fine dwelling on Market Street, adjacent to the northern end of the Moffatt-Ladd gardens. Although the house still stands, it has been severely altered from its original appearance. As originally built, the house exemplified perfectly the proportions and size of the typical pre-Revolutionary Portsmouth gambrel-roofed house.

Patch Collection

100

100. Built about 1743 by joiner Jonathan Low, this charmingly diminutive gambrel-roofed house stood until the mid-1880s at the corner of Court and Washington Streets. Its tiny size—twenty-seven feet square—resulted from the fact that it was built on a widow's one-third share of a larger lot of land. The equally-small Samuel Johnson house, which was being demolished at the time this photograph was made, stood on the western third of the same lot and was separated from the Low House by a five-foot alleyway. Despite its small size, the Low House was occupied by two families for many years during the 1800s.

Although the Low and Johnson houses were removed in the 1880s and their sites occupied by two apartment houses about 1900, the two newer houses have now been removed in their turn.

Patch Collection

101

101. This remarkable dwelling, a veritable village under one roof, had a history as long and interesting as the building itself. The first portion of the house, the section on the right, was built about 1740 by Colonel Nathaniel Meserve on the south shore of the North Mill Pond outlet, not far from the milldam. Meserve's shipyard was at the rear of the house, and here the Colonel constructed the famed fifty-gun *America* for the Royal Navy in 1749. Meserve died from smallpox at the second siege of Louisburg in 1758, along with a tragic number of the Piscataqua carpenters he commanded there. His house then passed into the hands of the wealthy Englishman Peter Livius, who constructed the North Milldam in 1764 and moved to a nearby house built for him by the noted joiner Michael Whidden III.

The Meserve House was bought shortly before 1770 by Colonel George Boyd, who had previously been foreman of a local ropewalk and who had suddenly and mysteriously become wealthy. Boyd enlarged the house, adding the portion in the center, which contained an elaborate formal parlor. The property of the mansion then extended south to Deer Street, and was bordered by water not only on the north, but also on the since-filled eastern side. On this extensive and beautiful tract Boyd laid out one of the finest gardens in New England, enclosing the plantings with an elaborate white fence whose posts were surmounted by carved grenadiers' heads. An early and anonymous painting of the house and garden is in the possession of the Phillips Exeter

Academy. Even at that time, the estate was sufficiently large and imposing to be locally referred to as the "White Village."

The house remained in the Boyd family until 1832, when it was purchased by the energetic shipbuilder George Raynes. Raynes added still another portion to the house at the far left, bringing the entire length of the building to about one hundred feet. The shipyard behind the house continued to operate until the late nineteenth century, producing scores of excellent vessels. The house was removed about 1938.

Patch Collection

102. The typical Portsmouth gambrel-roofed house was a "double" house with two chimneys and a central hallway, and dated from the 1740s through the 1760s. This small central-chimney dwelling, built after 1783 by Nathaniel Dean of Exeter, provided an interesting exception to the general rule. It stood at the southwest corner of Fleet and Congress streets, and its front doorway—a Federal type inspired by that of the nearby Woodbury Langdon Mansion—faced Fleet Street.

Like all dwellings along the once-residential Congress Street, the Dean House succumbed to the demands of commerce during the nineteenth century. George M. Plumer opened his baker's shop in the house prior to 1860, and had thus been a fixture on Congress Street for some thirty years when this photograph was made between 1890 and 1895.

The building seen at the left of this photograph was a blacksmith and wheelwright's shop. The tiny store at the right—originally Plumer's grocery store—belonged to Wilbur I. Trafton, a watchmaker, jeweler, and sometime-electrician who installed the first telephone line in Portsmouth on May 9, 1879.

Patch Collection

102

103 

104 

103. A fine New England house stood until the 1950s at the corner of Congress and Middle streets in Portsmouth, on the opposite corner from the Public Library. This imposing mansion was built about 1750 by Charles Treadwell and his enterprising wife, Mary, for their son Jacob.

The house bore a strong exterior resemblance to the Moffatt-Ladd House on Market Street, differing from the latter mainly in its lack of the strong central focus that the Moffatt House achieves through the use of a doorway portico and an elaborated window treatment over the door. The original doorway treatment was partially destroyed by the Victorian hood that was placed on the house during the last quarter of the nineteenth century.

On the interior, the Treadwell and Moffatt-Ladd Houses differed considerably. The Treadwell House was laid out as the typical eighteenth-century "double" (two chimney) house, having a spacious central hallway or entry with two rooms on each side of the entry on each floor. Thus, the interior effect of the Treadwell House was less monumental than that of the Moffatt House, which uses the space that would ordinarily be occupied by entry, front parlor and chimney for a grand hall and staircase that rank as one of the most ambitious architectural conceptions of colonial America. The Treadwell House interiors were, nevertheless, extraordinarily impressive, the rooms having been sumptuously paneled and enriched with heavy modillioned cornices. The stairhall was highly reminiscent of that in the 1784 Langdon Mansion.

The Treadwell House was wantonly destroyed to provide room for a bowling alley.

Patch Collection

104. This large, outstanding house, probably built around the mid-eighteenth century, formerly stood on the southwest corner of Hanover and Vaughan streets.

The house was remarkable both for its size and its detailing. It had the proportions of a traditional Portsmouth hip-roofed house, but with an unusual third story. The high pitch of its roof was emphasized by dormers, whereas Portsmouth's other pre-Revolutionary three-story hip-roofed dwellings, the Moffatt-Ladd and Jacob Treadwell Houses, utilized various means to de-emphasize their rooflines.

The Brewster-Hill House boasted fine quality trim. The front doorway was particularly outstanding, having one of the few ogee pediments used in the Piscataqua region.

This magnificent house, which remained in the Hill family until about 1896, was removed about 1904 to give way to a telephone exchange.

Patch Collection

105

105. The Judge John Sherburne House, which formerly stood at the corner of Daniel and Bow streets, numbered among the many casualties of the 1920s, a decade that saw the callous destruction of much of the best of Portsmouth's architectural heritage. The building may have been built as early as 1760 by John Sherburne, who was Judge of Probate under the Crown. After the elder Sherburne's death in 1797, the house was occupied by his son John Samuel Sherburne, U.S. District Judge until his death in 1830. During the mid-nineteenth century and later, the house served as a sailors' boarding house. It was demolished in 1924. A gasoline station occupies the site.

The house shows traces of more than one architectural period. Its original form as a gambrel-roofed dwelling is evident, but the double chimneys on the west end are probably changes of about 1800. The same is true of the building's intricate main cornice, which derives from a plate in Asher Benjamin's 1798 book, *The Country Builder's Assistant*. The cupola may be original, and was probably placed on the house in emulation of the cupola of the 1716 Warner House next door—an architectural feature that had been part of the original design of that mansion.

Patch Collection

106

107

106. The somewhat nondescript exterior of the Manning House, which stood at the intersection of Manning Place and Water (Marcy) Street, belied the splendor within. While parts of the building bore internal evidence of an early eighteenth-century date, the structure was probably given its final U-shaped form at about the time of the Revolution by its well-to-do owner, Capt. Thomas Manning. At that time, several fireplaces were embellished with elaborately-carved mantelshelves bearing floral festoons of the type that may be attributed to local carver Ebenezer Dearing (1730-1791). A number of the rooms were handsomely paneled. Thus it was natural, when the house fell into decay just prior to 1920, that it was acquired by the local antique dealer Charles Stewart who undoubtedly removed and sold its fine woodwork.
Staples-Herald Collection

107. A Manning House interior.
Staples-Herald Collection

108. The ancient house and tree which once stood on Pleasant Street opposite Gates Street, and which shared the change and growth of centuries before their final demise, embodied the tradition and continuity that formerly characterized every street and locale of the old town of Portsmouth.

The house, said to have been built shortly after 1760 by the Rev. Dr. Samuel Haven, minister of the South Church, was originally a two-story gambrel-roofed dwelling. It was enlarged to a three-story hip-roofed Federal-style house shortly after 1800, at a time when Dr. Haven's numerous progeny were constructing elegant mansions of similar appearance in various parts of town.

The extensive Haven family, once among the most influential and wealthy in Portsmouth, ultimately disappeared from the town. Under a provision of the will of Dr. Haven's descendants, the ancestral home was deliberately taken down upon the death of the last family member.

Patch Collection

109 

110 

109. One of the outstanding Portsmouth brick houses stood until the 1920s on Islington Street, at the corner of Parker Street. This was the home of Robert Rice, a wealthy merchant whose capital financed many of Portsmouth's commercial ventures before 1850. The Rice House was built about 1816 on a lot of land that had formerly been part of the garden of Nathaniel Adams, and that Rice had purchased from the aging historian Adams at the then-astonishing price of $3,200.

Adams himself related an interesting anecdote concerning the Rice House in his *Annals of Portsmouth:*

> On Wednesday evening, the 20th of June, [1821], the town was visited with a severe thunder storm, attended with heavy rain. The lightning struck the house of Robert Rice, Esquire, on Islington Road. The spouts round the eaves of the house were filled with water, and overflowed in front of the house. The electric fluid appears to have been conducted by the rain to the current of water in the spouts, and in its descent, was attracted by the iron weights to the windows. It shattered the blinds, broke some of the glass, tore away a shutter, and forced it a considerable distance into the room. It then descended to the lower story, broke down some of the plaister of the wall, and was conducted along the bell-wire, which it melted, to the bell handle on the outside of the door, and passed off by the iron railing to the ground."

At the time of Rice's death in 1853, his estate was evaluated at over $188,000, and his substantial fortune, left to Rice's only surviving daughter Arabella, made her one of the wealthiest women in New England at the time.

Staples-Herald Collection

110. The dynamic quality of Federal period architecture is epitomized in this study of the stairhall of the 1799 John Peirce Mansion, recorded about 1900. The spiral stairway, a hallmark of post-Revolutionary American building, was brought to supreme perfection by the skilled joiners of the Piscataqua region. Examples of their mastery may be seen in several of Portsmouth's elegant Middle Street mansions. The joiner Asher Benjamin, who credited himself with the construction of the first such stair in New England (in the 1796 Hartford State House), helpfully published several books to aid his "brother joiners" in mastering the difficult geometry of such work.

The Peirce Mansion was the first fully-developed Federal-style dwelling in the Piscataqua region. Built by the energetic merchant John Peirce, whose estate totaled an incredible $103,000 at his death in 1814, this house was one of the showplaces of northern New England, and was similar in design to Boston-area houses designed by Charles Bulfinch. The curved settee seen in this photograph is among the outstanding pieces of surviving New England Federal furniture. It was built (probably by a local cabinetmaker) to fit the curved niche at the bottom of the stairs. It may be seen today in the Winterthur Museum in Delaware.

Patch Collection

111

111. This remarkable dwelling, shown in an early and much-retouched photograph, was one of the most sophisticated houses ever erected in Portsmouth. Constructed in 1813 by Jonathan Folsom (1785-1825), Portsmouth's most skilled contractor in the late Federal period, the house may well have been designed by its well-traveled builder. It stood on the western corner of Middle Street and Richards Avenue, and, in Folsom's own words, was "noted for its grand and romantic appearance." It was purchased in 1814 by merchant Thomas Haven. The fifteen-room house bore a striking resemblance to the "Octagon" in Washington, D.C., with which Folsom may well have been familiar. It was removed about 1880 to provide a site for the equally grand Victorian-style Sinclair House.

Folsom's extensive real estate speculations led him to erect many of Portsmouth's finest brick structures, several of which still survive. He also gained local fame as the constructor of the massive Alabama Shiphouse at the Navy Yard. Folsom became interested in granite construction at the birth of that new technology, and built the stone sea wall at the Isles of Shoals. His chief monument was the stone Unitarian Church in Portsmouth. During its completion he died from over-exertion.

Patch Collection

112

113

114

112. On Broad Street is the home of a self-made man. Benjamin Franklin Webster (1824-1916) came to Portsmouth from Epsom at the age of seventeen, and was apprenticed to carpenter Benjamin Norton. He mastered not only the trades connected with building construction, but, like many of his skillful contemporaries, became a proficient ship's joiner as well. Webster made his reputation as a builder by constructing such substantial structures as the Kearsarge Hotel and the Cabot Street School in the 1860s. He subsequently built many of the notable Victorian residences of Portsmouth, and, as his prosperity increased, became one of the city's wealthiest men and largest property owners.

In 1880, Webster constructed this house, which epitomizes its own era as perfectly as the grand Georgian or Federal mansions of Portsmouth typify theirs. Set amid beautifully landscaped grounds on the hilltop once known as "Rundlett's Mountain," the Webster House combines grandeur and good taste. Its flush-boarded walls provide a foil for the complexity of its bracketed ornamentation. In design, the house is a combination of the "Italianate" and "Renaissance revival" styles—the latter a late nineteenth century development that often lent its mannered elements to furniture design.

Inside, the house is extraordinarily sumptuous, making lavish use of walnut, mahogany, and gumwood. Yet, underlying all the intricacy of design and execution is a basic understanding born of long experience by a man grown wealthy, but still a master builder. In this photograph of about 1895, Webster himself sits proudly in his buggy, while his wife Sarah watches from atop the marble stairs. His daughter, Stella, poses in front of a bed of towering hollyhocks.

Patch Collection

113. It is easy to forget that the splendid Portsmouth mansions of the eighteenth century, some of which are restored to museum perfection today, continued to change and evolve during the years when they were the stylish homes of generations of occupants. The 1784 Governor John Langdon Mansion, today largely returned to its early appearance and opened to the public, is seen here as it appeared at the end of the Victorian era. Because of a post-Civil War stylistic revival, the rococo complexity of the gas chandelier and of the massive Chickering overstrung grand piano blend well with the rococo delicacy of the original carved woodwork and with the eighteenth-century Chippendale chair.

Patch Collection

114. This sumptuous boudoir, with its elegant rococo furnishings, its bordered wallpaper, and its studied obliteration of all empty spaces, would appear to epitomize the Victorian chamber. The experienced eye, however, will detect a few traces of an earlier style—a Georgian cornice or a colonial fireplace—hidden with almost complete success beneath the overlay of nineteenth century embellishments. This room is, in fact, a chamber in the Joseph Whipple House of about 1760 as it appeared in the 1890s. The manner in which the original character of the room is hidden attests to the vigor and self-assurance of the late nineteenth-century style.

Patch Collection

115

115. Even in a simple home, the Victorian parlor sometimes became extraordinarily elegant. This room utilized all the skills of the Italian marble-cutter and the English Parian-ware maker to become a veritable sculpture gallery. The photograph was probably made about 1890, but the decor of the room, carefully maintained by its elderly owners, reflects the taste of thirty or forty years earlier. The painting over the mantelpiece appears to be the work of the local artist and music teacher Thomas P. Moses, who flourished in the sixties and seventies. The grotesque fish above the picture, perhaps a type of sculpin, was probably carved from wood by some local craftsman or fisherman.

Patch Collection

116. "There are few men who were boys in Portsmouth at the period of which I write but will remember Wibird Penhallow and his sky-blue wheelbarrow. I find it difficult to describe him other than vaguely, possibly because Wibird had no expression whatever in his countenance. With his vacant white face lifted to the clouds, seemingly oblivious to everything, yet going with a sort of heaven-given instinct straight to his destination, he trundled that rattling wheelbarrow for many a year over Portsmouth cobblestones. He was so unconscious of his environment that sometimes a small boy would pop into the empty wheelbarrow and secure a ride without Wibird arriving at any very clear knowledge of the fact. His employment in life was to deliver groceries and other merchandise to purchasers. This he did in a dreamy, impersonal kind of way. It was as if a spirit had somehow got hold of an earthly wheelbarrow and was trundling it quite unconsciously, with no sense of responsibility." from: T.B. Aldrich, *An Old Town By the Sea* [1894 edition]

Aldrich's portrait of the wheelbarrow man, though perhaps accurately depicting Penhallow's customary demeanor, is misleadingly one-sided. Actually, he was more than just a member of Portsmouth's fraternity of porters, of whom some were employed by merchants and some, like Penhallow, labored independently. Surprisingly, the stolid Penhallow published Portsmouth's first town directories in 1821 and 1827, thus giving invaluable aid to the antiquarian and establishing a tradition that has continued to the present. He died on December 30, 1867, aged seventy-six.

Staples-Herald Collection

116

The People

117

118

117. The crews of the nineteenth-century sailing vessels were often an unruly lot, and required a man of iron will to command them. To judge by his face, Capt. Daniel Marcy was the man for the job. Marcy, orphaned at the age of twelve, first tasted salt water the next year when he signed for a voyage to Demarara in the West Indies. Throughout his youth and young manhood, Marcy followed the sea, first as a sailor and, after his twenty-first birthday, as a New Orleans shipmaster. He returned to his birthplace in Portsmouth in 1842 to oversee the construction of a vessel, and thereafter supervised the construction of a Portsmouth-built ship every year until the Civil War. Until 1852, Marcy routinely commanded the maiden voyage of each craft built under his direction. After the Civil War, he was instrumental in reviving the moribund shipbuilding business in Portsmouth, operating a flourishing shipyard east of Marcy Street, near the outlet of the South Mill Pond. In 1878, at about the time this portrait was made, Marcy constructed the 1,800-ton *Granite State*, the largest ship built at Portsmouth up to that time.

In 1854, Marcy returned from a southern trip to learn that he had unexpectedly been elected to the state legislature. He followed an active political life thereafter, becoming a United States congressman in 1863. He died in 1893, four days short of his eighty-fourth birthday.

Patch Collection

119

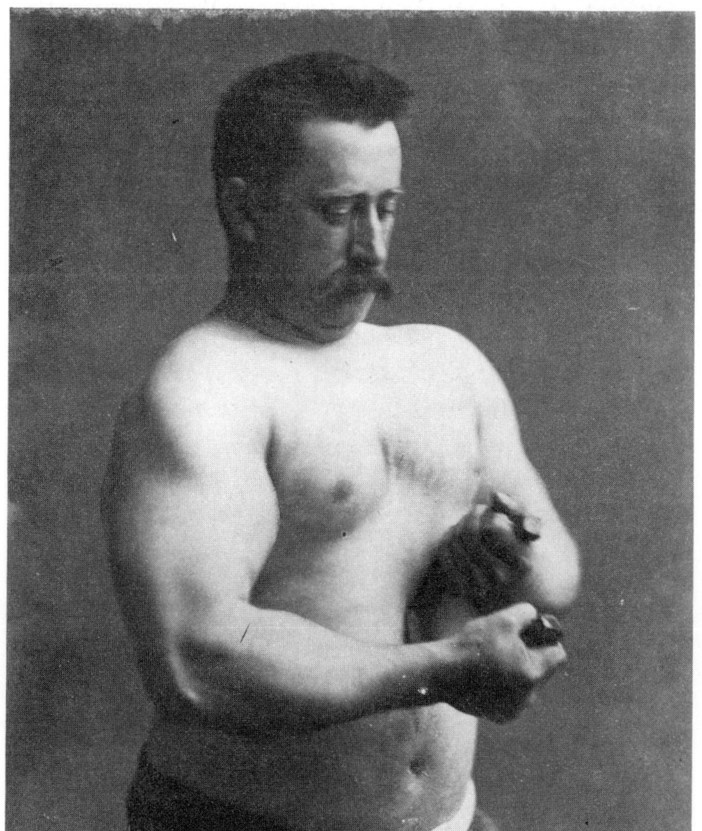

120

118. The man whose life extends from one century into the next is common enough, but rare indeed is the man whose lifespan touches three centuries. Such an individual was James Wood, who was born in Chivelstone, Devonshire, England, in 1796 and died in Portsmouth on December 22, 1900, aged 104 years and thirteen days. Wood was a tailor by trade, and continued active at his craft until about the time of his hundredth birthday. During his last years he carried on the business in his small eighteenth-century house that still stands on Jefferson Street. This photograph was made shortly before his death.

Patch Collection

119. His bulging muscles rendered even more awesome by the photographer's artful retouching, strongman Edward Stickney pits his strength against a worthy adversary. Even a man of Stickney's obvious powers would have a difficult time with the shoe of a draft horse, however, and the photographer has left no second negative to indicate which was the victor in this heroic contest.

Patch Collection

120. "Nellie" (Helen A.) Newell, daughter of Lafayette V. Newell, Portsmouth's leading photographer, strikes a typical Victorian pose about 1890.

Patch Collection

121 

122 

121. Photographer Lafayette V. Newell and his twin brother Albert M. (which is which?) pose for the camera during the 1890s.

Patch Collection

122. The life of Frank Jones, brewing magnate, railroad builder, insurance king and self-made man, has probably inspired more legends than that of any other Portsmouth individual. Even this portrait has two legends connected with it: it is said to be the only photograph that Jones ever permitted to be made of himself (untrue); it is claimed that Jones bought the photographer a special camera needed to make the oversized original of this portrait (possible but unlikely).

Jones' expansive life cannot be summarized easily. He was born in the country town of Barrington in 1832, and came to Portsmouth at age seventeen. He worked as a peddler in the tin and stove business of his brother Hiram, finally buying that enterprise when he was twenty-one. A few years later, the young man was able to purchase a modest brewing business, and from 1861 he began to devote his energies single-mindedly to its development. The time favored his success, and, as his Portsmouth business grew, he acquired an extensive interest in another brewery in South Boston. By the 1890s, when Jones sold his interests to an English syndicate, he had almost single-handedly built one of America's mightiest brewing empires.

Meanwhile, he had become president of the Boston and Maine Railroad, had built the far-famed Rockingham and

Wentworth hotels in Portsmouth and New Castle, and had pioneered in the establishment of several New Hampshire insurance companies when out-of-state underwriters, resenting New Hampshire's reformed insurance laws, ceased their operations. Locally, Jones had interests in a shoe company (largest in the world), a button factory (also the world's largest), several banks, water and electric companies, a theatre, and a seemingly endless list of other enterprises. Jones left an estate valued at more than five million dollars, but it was said of him that "he never made a dollar but what the city of Portsmouth benefited."

Patch Collection

123

123. Frank Jones did everything in a flamboyant manner, and saw to it that what he did was the best possible. A case in point was the "Frank Jones Rope-Pulling Team," which transformed the rugged pastime of the brewery hands into a championship sport. This photograph immortalizes not only the burly crew with their manager and captain, but also the heavy belt and line with which the team dragged innumerable scuffling opponents to an ignominious defeat.

Patch Collection

124

124. An often-repeated tale, probably nurtured by the legend-loving Frank Jones himself, relates that Jones' first trip to Portsmouth brought him to the Newington Road at about three o'clock in the morning. Arriving at the Wiggin Tavern at Gravelly Ridge, and finding no one awake, the seventeen-year-old lad spent the rest of the night in a shed by the stable. Jones never forgot his first night in the town that was to make his fortune, and eighteen years later he purchased the site of Wiggin's inn for his summer home.

Enclosed with beautifully fashioned stone walls, the thousand-acre grounds eventually included vegetable gardens, innumerable imported and exotic species of trees and plants, greenhouses, statuary, fountains, fish ponds, tennis courts, croquet lawns, and a large race track. Jones named the showplace "Maplewood Farm" because of the many trees he had set out along its roads. The farm became known as a place of resort for local people—"the Public Garden of Portsmouth."

The interior of one of Jones' half-dozen hothouses is seen here.

Patch Collection

125 

126 

125. One of the legendary figures of early twentieth-century Portsmouth, and a man whose name is still familiar on the city's streets today, was "Cappy" Stewart. Proprietor of an oyster saloon, keeper of a Water Street house of ill fame, and antique dealer *par excellence*, Charles H. Stewart participated in the evolution of Portsmouth from a nineteenth-century rough-and-tumble Navy depot to a twentieth-century mecca for the antiquarian and historian. Many of the historical artifacts that remain in Portsmouth today are there because of Stewart's interest, and conversely many of those that have left the town forever are gone because of his business enterprise. Stewart dealt not only in the odds-and-ends of the typical "antique" shop; he also sold to major museums and to the most discriminating private collectors. His stock in trade ranged from second-hand machinery to furniture and room interiors that represented the highest achievement of the eighteenth century Portsmouth craftsman. It was he who acquired and sold the woodwork of the John Wentworth House, now in the Metropolitan and Winterthur Museums. And, as this photograph reveals, it was he who somehow acquired the old 1792 Portsmouth handtub, which has been owned privately since the period of this picture. Despite his shrewdness as a businessman, however, Stewart is remembered by those who were young when he was old as a kindly and generous man.

Staples-Herald Collection

126. The faces of ancient men hold a strong fascination that early twentieth-century photographers felt keenly. Time and again, one comes upon negatives that record the lineaments of a generation that had witnessed much of the nineteenth century. Only two men in this photograph can be identified with certainty: Joseph Wiley Coleman (left rear), a carpenter born in 1823; and Daniel Mason (front center), born in 1821 and for many years a proprietor of a steam planing mill.

Patch Collection

127

127. Looking considerably more cheerful than his customer, a bootblack plies his trade at the alleyway east of Frank Jones' National Block on Congress Street. The picture probably dates from the first decade of the twentieth century.

Staples-Herald Collection

128

128. The modern dental patient can only be thankful for the advances of eighty years as he observes from this photograph how dentistry was practiced in the nineties. Even the dog in the lower foreground appears worried. The only light in the room was provided by the gas burner near the window. The dentist's treadle-powered drill was agonizingly slow and unsteady. Novocaine was unheard-of, but the patient requiring major surgery could be given nitrous oxide or laughing gas, as may be seen in the adjoining room. To judge by the decor of the office, the germ theory had not yet been applied in dentistry, or at least in this dentist's practice. Worst of all, however, each patient had an all-too-ample opportunity to anticipate his fate as he observed every detail of the operation on the patient that preceded him in the chair.

Patch Collection

129

130

129. With faces that record the labors and trials of much of the nineteenth century, the oldest men of Portsmouth pose for the camera in 1909. Virtually every individual in the group was alive when the courthouse steps on which they stand were laid down in 1836. By that year, some of the oldest men had already embarked on careers which, with the steadfastness characteristic of an earlier era, they were still usefully pursuing when the photographer caught their pictures. The life histories of these octogenarians and nonagenarians were so diverse that only the common bond of age united them. Their careers had ranged from farmer to undertaker, from painter to blacksmith, from shipbuilder to mayor. The four men in the lower left of the photograph present a typical cross-section of the group: Amos Pearson (with cane), music teacher and florist; Daniel McIntire, toll gatherer at the Portsmouth Bridge; Edward Moulton, a joiner at the Navy Yard; Samuel W. Lolley, a fisherman. The two oldest men in the group, John

131

132

E. Butler and Benjamin M. Parker, both in their nineties, are seated in the Duryea automobile.

Patch Collection

130. A vine-covered cottage, a flourishing vegetable garden, plenty of old-fashioned chairs on the lawn and piazza, and friends who remember the better days that once were—what more could an elderly gentleman wish on a late summer afternoon?

Patch Collection

131. These five young dudes, obviously aware of their own impressive elegance, pose with a pony cart at Mechanic Street in 1886.

Patch Collection

132. Somehow looking older than their modern-day counterparts, the members of the Portsmouth High School graduating class of 1897 pose on the steps of the 1836 Court House.

Patch Collection

133

134

133. The infinite detail in this almost-candid photograph of the Plains schoolhouse in Portsmouth is fascinating even to those whose memories do not extend back to the days of the one-room school. The brick building was opened on January 3, 1846, and was probably about a half-century old when this picture was made. The kindly visage of Henry Wadsworth Longfellow, almost a patron saint to the nineteenth-century schoolchild, looks down benignly from the back of the room. One can well imagine the faces of Washington and Lincoln returning his gaze from behind the teacher's cluttered desk in the foreground.

Patch Collection

134. One of the forgotten phenomena of the late 1800s was the burgeoning of "women's clubs" throughout New England. Such organizations were usually founded on a generalized plan, and sought mainly to nurture companionship and common interests among the members. Here the members of the "Friendship Club" of Portsmouth gather for a group portrait in 1888.

Patch Collection

135. The Kearsarge Flute and Drum Band, one of several independent musical groups active in Portsmouth before the turn of the century, are recorded on the steps of the North Church.

Patch Collection

136. Portsmouth before the turn of the century was filled with athletic clubs and competitive teams. Here the "Red Stocking Base Ball Club" poses for photographer L.V. Newell in 1886. Obviously self-equipped, the men wear a somewhat motley selection of clothes, even varying markedly in their all-important stockings. Nevertheless, the team maintained its own headquarters on Congress Street and was probably better organized than most clubs of the period.

Patch Collection

135

136

137

138

137. The Portsmouth High School football team of 1891 posed with studied nonchalance on the photographer's grass rug, with a backdrop that seemed to place them simultaneously in classical Rome and a rustic flower garden. Disregard for padding made football a notoriously rough sport in those days, but the team compensated for its lack of protective clothing with luxurious Kimball sweaters.

Patch Collection

138. The strong resemblance between members of Portsmouth's athletic teams in the nineties was no coincidence, for that period was the heyday of the legendary Woods family. Composed of eight full brothers and sisters and seven more half brothers and sisters, the family was capable of fielding a formidable team. Most of the male Woodses excelled in the rugged sports of the era, participating both in high school and as members of various independent athletic groups. Four of the Woods brothers can be identified in this photograph of a high school football team: three have a black "P" on their sweaters, and the fourth reclines in front of the group.

Patch Collection

139. When a young baseball star graduated from high school, his career was not necessarily halted at its zenith. The Portsmouth Athletic Club, which maintained its own impressive headquarters in the Salter House on Court Street, offered a welcome to any young or not-so-young sportsman.

Patch Collection

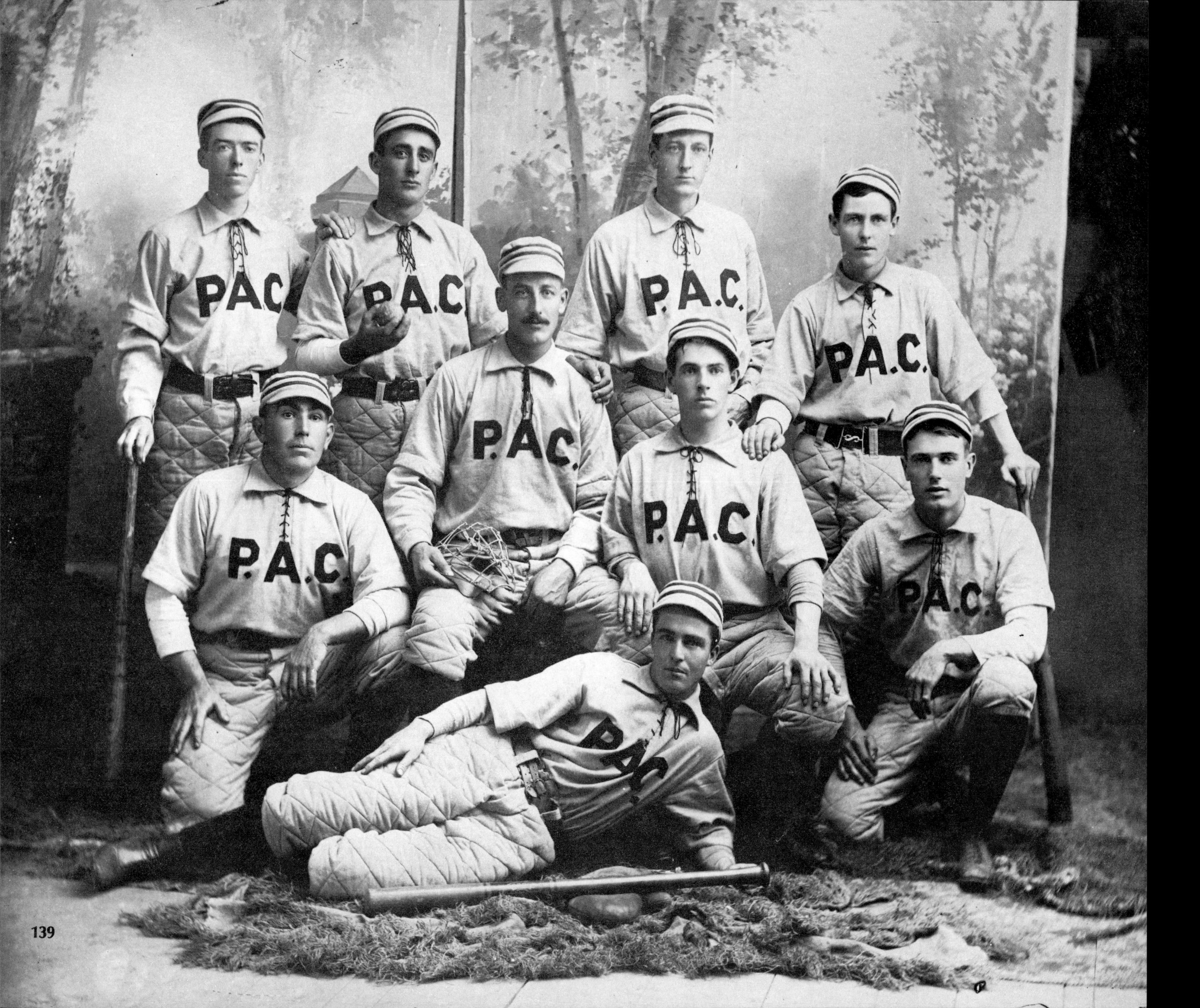

139

140

Firemen
and Other Fighters

141

142

140. The men of Willard J. Sampson Hook and Ladder Company, Number 1, pose in front of their festooned wagon sometime in the nineties. "H.&L. No. 1" had long been the only ladder company in the city, having borne the proud name of "Garibaldi Company" during the 1860s.

Patch Collection

141. The dreadful fires which swept Portsmouth's tightly packed neighborhoods about 1800 could not have been assuaged in any measure by the town's fire-fighting equipment. One of the newest pieces of apparatus available was this fire engine. Although the machine embodies both superb workmanship for the times and a marked technological advance over earlier hand-tubs, the modern fireman would blanch at the prospect of trying to contain a raging blaze in a thoroughfare like Gates Street with such a pumper as this. The problem was compounded by the fact that eighteenth-century engines had no suction hose; the cisterns at their ends were supplied by water brigades armed with the universal leather fire buckets, filled at whatever well or pump might be near.

This machine, built in 1792, was number 121 of a series constructed by Richard Mason of Philadelphia, who began making fire engines in 1768. Mason is credited with inventing the "Philadelphia" model engine, having its levers at the ends rather than the sides. The old machine was somehow acquired by the local antique dealer Charles Stewart, and is today owned by a private collector.

Patch Collection

142. The science of fire-fighting had advanced astonishingly in the following century. On December 30, 1864, the city acquired its first steam fire engine. By 1890, when this photograph was made, the fire department included four steamers, two extinguisher companies, one hook and ladder company, and a supply wagon company.

This photograph shows the gleaming Kearsarge pumper, No. 3, pulled out in front of the Court Street fire house, next to the present Central Fire Station. The scene may have been in September, at the time of Portsmouth's annual Fireman's Muster, for the nozzles and smokestack of the engine are adorned with bouquets of fresh flowers.

Patch Collection

143. The proverbial visiting firemen turned out in force in Portsmouth in 1883. To judge by the traditional broom held by the man on the wagon, these visitors from Keene must have made a "clean sweep" of Portsmouth's firemen's muster in that year. Perhaps they won their victory in a foot race pulling the piece of equipment with which they are posed—the hose reel belonging to Portsmouth's Kearsarge engine, Number 3.

Patch Collection

144. Seldom did two spirited fire horses and their proud crew have such an audience! The firebells rang at the very moment when the bands struck up a martial air for the 1913 Memorial Day parade and began to pass through Market Square. The horses stepped to the quick hitch, the boiler was fired, and Engine Three rumbled out into Congress Street a moment ahead of the marchers.

Patch Collection

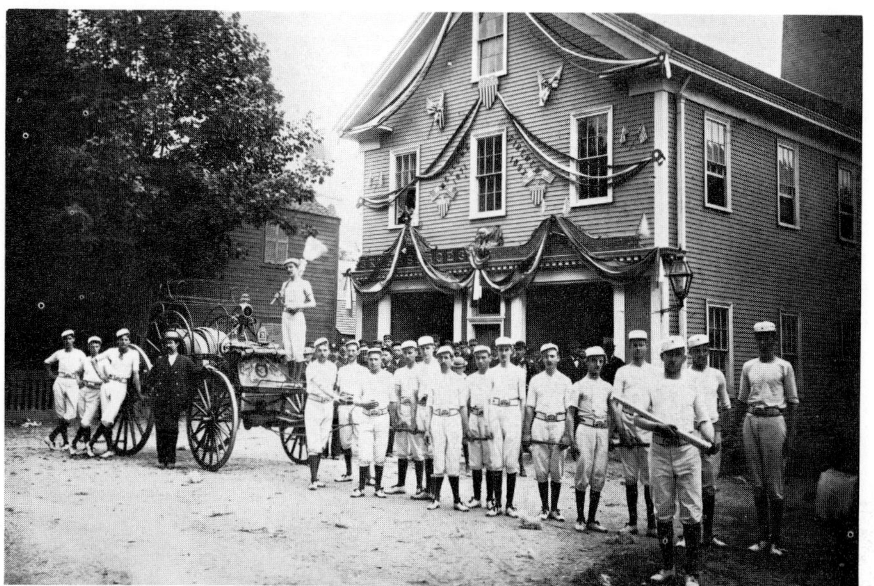

143

144

145

146

145. Looking capable and businesslike despite their lack of firefighting suits, the men of Kearsarge Engine Company, Number 3, were recorded by the camera in front of the Court Street engine house on May 8, 1879.

Patch Collection

146. Garbed in their distinctive white coats and helmets, the fire department's Board of Engineers—equivalent to today's chief and deputy chiefs—posed for the photographer in 1915. In the center is Chief Engineer William F. Woods who combined longterm service as fire chief with proprietorship of a harness business in the Rogers Building on Congress Street.

Patch Collection

147. "Remember the Maine! Recruits Wanted." These were fighting words in 1898, before "the war to end all wars" dimmed forever the aura of chivalry and adventure that had accompanied military service. Here the First Regiment, Company A, New Hampshire Volunteers, stand confidently on the steps of the 1836 courthouse. The young men in the background with civilian clothes are undoubtedly new recruits who have just signed up.

Patch Collection

148. The war with Spain brought its share of tragedies on both sides. There is little joy to be seen in the faces of these men—Spanish prisoners who were barracked at the Portsmouth Navy Yard. In July, 1898, two days after the surrender of Admiral Cervera's fleet at Guantanamo, Cuba, the Portsmouth yard received an emergency order to construct a prison camp for some 1,600 men. Within six days a veritable army of workmen had thrown up a ten-foot stockade enclosing eight large barracks for prisoners, four cell-houses, three mess halls (each two hundred feet long), one wash house, and a latrine, as well as eight more barracks for the marine guard and houses for army and navy officers. The first complement of 1,000 prisoners arrived just as the hasty work was being completed.

The men arrived in woeful condition, weary, feverish, and undernourished. Local accounts, which we can hope were honest, state that the prisoners benefited greatly from their weeks at Portsmouth. They soon recovered sufficiently to engage in mock bull fights and other sports, including that of fishing from the ledges of Seavey's Island.

Patch Collection

147

148

149

150

149. In September, 1898, the great steamship *City of Rome* arrived in Portsmouth harbor. Almost exactly two months after their arrival, the Spanish prisoners of war, except for thirty who died and were buried on Seavey's Island, embarked for Santander, Spain.

Patch Collection

150. In 1808 Portsmouth granted the Federal government a lot near the South School, sixty by ninety-six feet, for the construction of a gun house. The arsenal was evidently a one-story structure at first, enlarged to two stories during the nineteenth century. It remained, largely disused, until about the time of World War I.

Patch Collection

151. A survival from an earlier period of warfare, the stone and timber blockhouse at Fort McClary, Kittery Point, towers incongruously over the mighty hammered granite walls below. Built in 1845-46, the blockhouse served only for small-arms defense of the shores below the bluff. The brick guardhouse at the left, augmented by the buttressed magazine in the center and the barracks at the right, served a similar purpose. At the time of the Civil War, however, the Federal government began an ambitious plan to build a great stone fortress on the site. The guns of Fort McClary, crossing fire with those of the similarly fortified Fort Constitution in New Castle, would effectively seal Portsmouth harbor against naval attack.

The same war that inspired these defensive works, however, rendered them obsolete before their completion.

The guns of earlier warships had lacked the accuracy to pound such ramparts as those of Fort McClary in a single area—the only way to break them effectively. Before the end of the Civil War, heavy-caliber rifled naval guns were developed, having superb accuracy and increased range. They were capable of firing projectiles of great penetrating power. Such armament was immediately recognized as fatal to even the strongest vertical-walled fort, and work was immediately stopped on all such coastal works.

Staples-Herald Collection

151

152

152. A monument to an outmoded war technology, the granite ramparts of Fort Constitution in New Castle stand uncompleted and useless in this photograph of the 1880s. The stone fortifications at the water's edge, begun in 1863 and continued briefly after the Civil War, were intended to provide emplacements for three tiers of guns, and to encircle Fort Point outside of the perimeters of the older forts at the location. Improvements in ballistics rendered the proposed vertical walls vulnerable; labor ceased before the first gun tier was completed.

Fort Point, the location of these Cyclopean ruins, was one of the first fortified sites in the Piscataqua region. There were earthworks and "great guns" on the point early in the seventeenth century, and in 1666 a more regular fortification was constructed. From the late 1600s until the Revolution, the installation was called Fort William and Mary, and was alternately improved and neglected. In 1774, New Hampshire insurgents captured the fort in the first American aggressive action of the Revolution. Extensive works of brick, stone and earth were constructed on the point in 1808, and the name Fort Constitution was applied to the garrison at that time, if not earlier. After the burst of activity inspired by the Civil War, the fort was almost totally abandoned until modern disappearing guns, manned by the Coast Artillery, were installed during the Spanish War. The site is now a Coast Guard base.

Staples-Herald Collection

153

154

153. The Martello Tower, a little west of the fort, was erected during the War of 1812 as extra protection against an expected British naval assault. When no enemy appeared, the tower was allowed to fall into disrepair, as this photograph amply attests.

Patch Collection

154. Only once did old Fort Constitution briefly return to life between the cessation of construction activities at the end of the Civil War and the installation of coastal defense guns just before 1900. That occasion was the celebration of the two-hundredth anniversary of New Castle's existence as a separate town. On August 17, 1893, the bells of New Castle proclaimed the event, and a battery of field guns set upon the bluff overlooking the river began to thunder a national salute.

Patch Collection

155. Members of Company 124, United States Coast Artillery, drape themselves across the old portcullis gate of Fort Constitution in 1902; several baseball gloves among the group attest to their major employment at the fort.

The portcullis gate was part of the 1808 walls of Fort Constitution. These ramparts were constructed as a result of extensive defense appropriations made available in that year when Congress voted to improve coastal defenses in preparation for what was correctly supposed to be an inevitable war with Britain. Though poorly maintained in later years, the walls still survive in part.

Patch Collection

A Day
in the Country

157

158

156. Seeming to defy all known laws of balance, the three-story conveyance survived in Rye as late as 1900. One can only marvel at the temerity of the roof-top riders, whose combined weight of over a thousand pounds must have occasioned some terrifying lateral lurches of the leather-slung coach even if the vehicle did not actually capsize. Accidents did, in fact, sometimes occur: in one instance in 1890, over-eager employees of the famous S.S. Pierce grocery house in Boston were spilled in the dust as the over-burdened and top-heavy coach left the North Hampton depot for a day's holiday at the Farragut Hotel.

In the 1880s, the classic Concord coach, built by the New Hampshire firm of Abbott and Downing, became the standard shuttle vehicle between the North Hampton, Greenland, and Portsmouth depots and the resort hotels and boarding houses of railless Rye and Rye Beach. The proud Farragut Hotel, in fact, boasted a four-horse Tally-Ho that is said to have cost nearly $2,000—about twice the price of the standard hotel coach. This picturesque if somewhat jolting and dusty mode of transportation flourished until the turn of the century, when the electric cars from Portsmouth ushered in a more modern era in transportation.

The group in this photograph is aboard one of the brown-painted Concord coaches of the Adams Drake line, and awaits departure from the boarding house of S.W. Foss at Rye Beach.

Patch Collection

157. These two ladies, fashionably attired and seated in a jaunty gig, prepare to enjoy the sea air near Rye Beach about 1890.

Patch Collection

158. These dandies, with their blazers and caps, are a group of barbers at a picnic in 1886. The scene may be at Chauncey's Creek in Kittery, a favorite place for outings.

Patch Collection

159. Founded September 10, 1885, the Portsmouth Athletic Club was subdivided into smaller units to satisfy every sporting interest. Here the Mascotte Boat Club of the P.A.C. enjoys an outing on Chauncey's Creek, Kittery Point, Maine, about 1890. The big ten-oar boat, flagship of the P.A.C. fleet, was probably a converted captain's gig from some defunct naval vessel.

Patch Collection

159

160

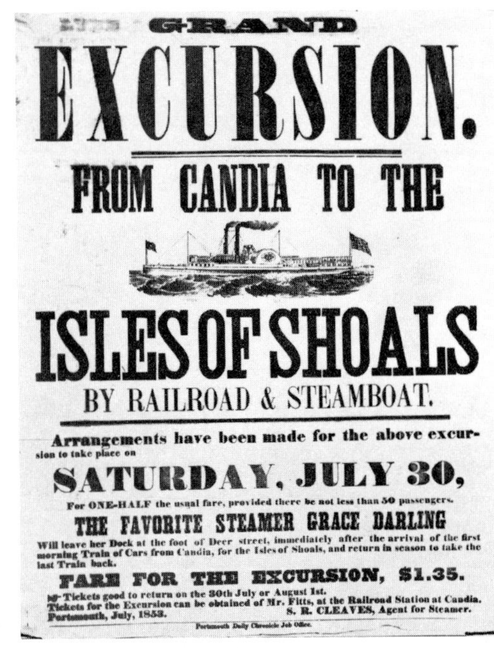
GRAND

EXCURSION.

FROM CANDIA TO THE

ISLES OF SHOALS

BY RAILROAD & STEAMBOAT.

Arrangements have been made for the above excursion to take place on

SATURDAY, JULY 30,

For ONE-HALF the usual fare, provided there be not less than 50 passengers.

THE FAVORITE STEAMER GRACE DARLING

Will leave her Dock at the foot of Deer street, immediately after the arrival of the first morning Train of Cars from Candia, for the Isles of Shoals, and return in season to take the last Train back.

FARE FOR THE EXCURSION, $1.35.

Tickets good to return on the 30th July or August 1st.
Tickets for the Excursion can be obtained of Mr. Fitts, at the Railroad Station at Candia.
Portsmouth, July, 1853. S. R. CLEAVES, Agent for Steamer.

Portsmouth Daily Chronicle Job Office.

161

160. Steam, nineteenth-century man's great servant, made possible such wonders as the excursion advertised in this 1853 broadside—a one-day trip from the inland town of Candia to the Isles of Shoals and back. Because of the enterprise of the Laighton family at the Shoals, the islands were becoming popular not only for brief outings, but for extended summer vacations as well. In 1848, Thomas Laighton and Levi Thaxter had opened the Appledore House, touted as the first resort hotel between Eastport, Maine, and Nantucket, Massachusetts. Though the eighty-room hotel boasted spacious parlors and a two-hundred foot piazza, visitors did not partake of its amenities without some hazard: until 1873 the Appledore had no piers, and tourists were ferried ashore, a distance of some fifty yards, by salty Shoals fishermen. The farmers' families of Candia had probably had their fill of the sea by the end of July 30, 1853.

Patch Collection

161. The population of the Isles of Shoals fluctuated greatly through the years, possibly rising to as many as 600 people (some have said 1,000) before 1650, and falling to as few as forty by the Revolution. In 1800, according to Dr. Jedidiah Morse, the Shoals supported 112 persons. Until the mid-nineteenth century, the islands' inhabitants subsisted almost solely by fishing. The opening of the Appledore Hotel radically changed the economy.

In 1872, John R. Poor of Massachusetts purchased Star Island and began to construct the Oceanic House.

The former inhabitants of the island moved to the mainland, and their picturesque cottages were removed to provide room for the rambling hotel.

This photograph, made during the 1880s, shows Star Island almost as it appeared when Poor completed his work, except that the original Oceanic House, which burned in its second season, had been replaced by the somewhat nondescript structure seen here.

Patch Collection

162

162. A number of stories, all uncomplimentary to the godless Shoalers, relate the demise of the 1720 wooden meeting house which preceded the sturdy stone structure at Gosport. The most scurrilous of these published accounts depicts the building "wantonly set on fire about 1790 by a party of drunken fishermen, who held a wild revel by its light while it was burning." Less sensational versions suggest more realistically that the house was merely dismantled and its timber consumed for fuel by the wood-poor islanders; and one apologist has stated that the building took fire from an over-heated stove. In any case, the event shocked the pious Society for the Propagation of the Gospel, which had been intermittently supplying Gosport with ministers throughout the eighteenth century. S.P.G. officials began to watch the backsliding Shoalers narrowly, and were scandalized at their findings. One minister calculated that the consumption of rum by the men of Star Island in a three-month period averaged twelve and three-quarter gallons apiece; another account mentions a solitary fisherman who heroically consumed forty gallons in twelve months.

Thus it was that the Rev. Dr. Jedidiah Morse recommended that a new meeting house be constructed of stone, noting that "it will be imperishable" even when exposed to the untrustworthy islanders. In his dedication sermon of November 24, 1800, the Rev. Dr. Morse stated with holy satisfaction, *"The inhabitants can not burn it for fuel."*

The people of Gosport affixed the codfish weather vane to the chapel tower in 1859. The town records (which must have been kept by the minister) express the uncertain but eternal hope: "May their own hearts yield to the breathings of the Divine Spirit as that vane does to the wind!" The wooden tower seen in this photograph of about 1890 blew down in 1892, and was immediately rebuilt of stone by Oscar Laighton.

Patch Collection

163 

164 

163. The first lighthouse on barren White Island was built in 1821. This light had ten white and five red lamps of the early type, with polished spherical or parabolic reflectors that focused the beams seaward. This tower was replaced in 1859 by the forty-six-foot lighthouse which appears as a distant speck in this photograph. The new structure was equipped with one of the early Fresnel lights brought to this country from France. The new illuminating system, which used a series of concentric cut-glass prisms to concentrate the rays of a single intense light source, was far more powerful than the older reflector lamps, but was likewise far more costly.

White Island light is particularly exposed to storms. Langdon B. Parsons, in his *History of Rye,* records that even the new tower was not beyond the reach of the sea: heavy storms threw kelp as high as the lantern gallery, seventy-eight feet above water level.

Patch Collection

164. In the winter of 1863-64, Oscar and Cedric Laighton constructed the "cottage" in the center of this photograph as a retirement home for their parents. The house overlooked the Appledore Hotel tennis courts, and, like the other buildings in the photograph, nestled close to the rambling, three-part structure (just out of the range of the camera on the right).

The cottage later became the well-known residence of poetess Celia Thaxter. Many reminiscences of the soirees conducted there by Mrs. Thaxter have been transmitted through the years. One account, written by a woman who had been a young girl in the 1890s, recalled that "in the evenings we had reading aloud or recitations by her or by some of the literary guests. The room was dim and mysterious, lighted only by a lamp on the piano or by her side. She would read us weird stories, or the adventures of the early settlers on the island . . . ."

A disastrous fire in 1914 swept away the hotel, the Thaxter cottage, and the other structures in this photograph.

Patch Collection

165

165. A contemporary describes the gruesome events which transpired in this unassuming cottage:

"On Wednesday night March 5, 1873, the quaint weather-beaten house on Smutty Nose Island, Isles of Shoals, represented in this picture, was the scene of a double murder the brutality of which is almost unparalleled in the annals of crime.

"Mr. John Hontvet and his wife; Matthew Hontvet, his brother; Ivan Christensen and his wife Anethe; Karen Christensen; and Louis Wagner, the murderer, were the only occupants of the fishing hamlet during the winter of '73, all occupying the house shown in this picture. The men were fishermen. On the night of March 5 the three women were left alone on the island, the men having gone to Portsmouth with fares of fish and to bait their trawls.

"On the following morning Hontvet and his men, save Wagner, early set sail for the fishing grounds. They hastened to the silent and apparently deserted house, the doors of which stand open wide. A horrible scene is presented. In the bedroom the ghastly form of Anethe mangled out of all human semblance lay stretched upon the floor. The house has two tenements divided by a partition, through which there are no doors. In the east bedroom was found the body of Karen, face down, with eleven wounds upon the head; a tightly-tied handkerchief about the neck.

"From Mr. Ingebretson, a fisherman living on Appledore, it was learned that Mrs. Hontvet had escaped from the murderer, and nearly frozen, was at his home. It was also now learned that Louis Wagner, their companion and fellow fisherman, and suitor for the hand of Karen, was the murderer.

"The authorities at Portsmouth were immediately notified and the search for Wagner began. His bloody clothes were found in an out-house on Water Street, and himself tracked to Boston where he was apprehended less than 24 hours after committing this most causeless and atrocious murder. His stealing a boat at Portsmouth and rowing to the Shoals and then rowing back again into Little Harbor—where he abandoned the boat, and his crawling across the stringers of the New Castle bridges, which were being repaired, were clearly proved against him at the preliminary hearings and trial, and resulted in his being executed at Thomaston, Maine, June 25, 1876.

"Wagner's motive was to get possession of a sum of money known to be in the house at the time of the murder. He obtained the paltry sum of $16." (Excerpts from "The Smutty Nose Tragedy," circa 1876, by "J.R.C.")

Patch Collection

166

167

166. Scores of Portsmouth-bound summer travelers clung to the running boards of an open car in 1917, at the height of the trolley era in the New Hampshire seacoast region. The scene is at Lang's Corner, Rye, one of the principal stopping points of the electric cars. In the background is the "Cape Cod" house of E.W. Lang. The Portsmouth Electric Railway, which opened its Rye extension in 1899, was run by the Boston and Maine Railroad, and provided the only rail transportation that the coastal community of Rye ever enjoyed. With a solicitude for natural beauty that has become increasingly rare, the railroad cooperated with the Rye selectmen in laying the tracks and overhead wires in a fashion that would minimize the cutting or pruning of trees along the right-of-way. Rye thereby gained a mode of public transportation that was convenient to the townsman, pleasant to the rider, and beneficial to the hotel owner. The line gave way to buses in 1925.

Patch Collection

167. The maintenance of an electric railway, from power plant to railbeds, was a full-time job. The Atlantic Shore Line Railway, the major system linking Portsmouth, Dover, Sanford, Kennebunk, and Biddeford, used a number of service cars and repair crews to maintain its extensive right-of-way. This photograph of about 1910 shows the installation of a new trolley wire, which can be seen running from the pole at the left past the man on the roof of the work car, and thence to the reel in the box car.

Patch Collection

168. The Sunday school picnic, a major social activity in the nineteenth century, is here seen in full flower. The excursion car has been pulled onto a siding at Stratham's Bayside Station while the scholars and their chaperones, from St. John's Church in Portsmouth, prepare for the day's outing. In the center of the group stands the popular Rev. Henry Emerson Hovey, rector of St. John's from 1883 until 1909.

Patch Collection

169. Members of the Masonic Knights Templar, looking very martial with their swords and uniforms, pose in front of the Portsmouth depot on Deer Street.

Patch Collection

168

169

170

170. Three serious young men, two of them suitably accoutered in dusters, pose with a chain-driven 1902 Winton. One wonders what daring exploit of the goggled and gauntletted driver has spattered the new machine with so much mud—and cost the automobile its left headlight glass.

Patch Collection

171. These gentlemen, obviously enjoying a country ride in their big touring car, have taken advantage of the perfect location for their companion photographer to record a bit of self-mockery. The picture was made in 1914.

Patch Collection

PIGS
for
SALE

SASHES.BLI
WINDOWS

A Miscellany

172. Portsmouth, like many northern coastal cities which had enjoyed firm mercantile ties with the South, retained some degree of sympathy for the Confederacy throughout the Civil War. The viewpoint of the "Copperheads," as southern sympathizers were called, was given expression by the Portsmouth newspaper, *States and Union.* On April 10, 1865, a drunken crowd, excited by news of the surrender of Lee's army at Richmond, gathered in front of the *States and Union* office on the northeast corner of Daniel and Penhallow Streets. As the *New Hampshire Gazette* recounts:

> a large and excited crowd soon gathered about the establishment, some clamoring for the proprietor, others crying "clean out the office," and yet others to "hang him," "string him up," and other like threatening language . . . . The crowd, frenzied with the glorious Union news and the excitement of the day, would listen to nothing but the promise of the appearance of Foster, the editor, to throw out *with his own hands* the ensign of Freedom.
>
> At last, this individual, pale with fear or rage, and well nigh overcome by the sight of about two thousand determined men, appeared at the window of his counting room, and with apparent reluctance put out his flag, giving it a slight toss with his hand; which not satisfying the majority of the crowd, they instantly demanded from him a speech . . . .
>
> But from some cause he (Foster) immediately disappeared, (it is said through a back door, taking his books,) which was the signal for a change of programme with the excited multitude.
>
> In less time than we are occupied in writing this, the office was completely riddled of type, presses, press boards, ink, paper, and everything connected with a printing establishment,—all thrown out of the windows into the street below. The Mayor appearing shortly after, and reading the riot act, the crowd dispersed.

Patch Collection

173. On April 15, 1865, Portsmouth was plunged into shock and grief by the announcement of Lincoln's death. The city bells tolled for the rest of the day, flags were dropped to half mast, business was suspended, and the Navy Yard was closed for five days.

On Monday forenoon, April 17, a public meeting was held in Market Square, presided over by ex-Governor Ichabod Goodwin. A contemporary account described the occasion, which is recorded in this early stereoscope photograph:

> A stand was erected in front of the Athenaeum, and very tastefully draped with mourning emblems—black and white festoons below, with a portrait of Mr. Lincoln, surmounted by a shield above, and the mottoes, "The Lord gave, and the Lord hath taken away," and "We mourn our beloved and honored Chief Magistrate, Abraham Lincoln."

On the following Wednesday a funeral procession was formed, with participation "more general than has marked any occasion in our record." Every dignitary from every available organization participated, with bands, carriages, and marchers forming a column half a mile in length and numbering between 1,200 and 1,400 people. The focal point of the procession was a "Car of the monumental order," more than fourteen feet long, with a gambrel-shaped roof supported by columns and surmounted by six black and white plumes. The massive vehicle, heavily draped in somber fabric, was drawn by six black horses. At about two o'clock in the afternoon the procession returned to Market Square, where "an auditory of not far from 3,000 stood quietly during the whole of the following service, and generally as still as if within the walls of a church."

Staples-Herald Collection

174. Portsmouth has a long tradition of celebrating the anniversary of the first New Hampshire settlement in 1623. For more than a hundred years, such celebrations have been marked by a "Return of the Sons" of the town from their homes throughout the country. Returning Portsmouth natives in 1873 were greeted by this banner at the South Mill bridge reminding them, in the words of John Howard Payne's ever-popular song, "There is no place like home."

Staples-Herald Collection

175. This gathering of vessels, lying in the outer harbor of the Piscataqua below the ramparts of Fort McClary, signals the end of one of the most daring and tragic exploratory ventures in American history. The Lady Franklin Bay Expedition, or the Greely Expedition as it was more popularly called, began in 1881 as part of the United States' contribution to the first International Polar Year (1882-1883). Commanded by Lieutenant Adolphus W. Greely of Newburyport, the venture was scheduled to establish a long-term outpost at Lady Franklin Bay, at about eighty-two degrees north latitude, drawing upon an open seam of coal at that point for fuel. The expedition would then make scientific observations throughout 1882, during the summer of which it would be resupplied by a relief ship. It would return on board a second relief ship in 1883.

All went well at first. The crowning triumph of the exploration was the attainment, in June 1882, of the record for northernmost penetration into the arctic by a three-man party from the main camp. Tragedy began in August, 1882, unbeknown to the expedition's members, when the first relief ship was deterred by ice some 200 miles short of the camp. Incredibly, the second relief ship sent a year later, was not only stopped but was crushed by the ice, leaving the Greely men totally abandoned beyond the normal limits of their supplies. No rescue was possible for still another year, until the summer of 1884.

Meanwhile, according to prearranged plan, the Greely men began to work their way southward when the second relief ship failed to arrive. After great hardship, the men found a small cache of supplies left for them previously, and established a camp in a desperate attempt to survive the deadly arctic night. Their numbers began to dwindle, and the minds and bodies of the survivors steadily weakened. In May, the men finally reached the end of their rations and prepared to die. Later investigations showed that some, none of whom seem to have survived, were driven to can-

173

174

175

176

177

nibalize their dead comrades.

In the same May, a relief squadron, shown here upon its return, steamed northward for a final attempt to rescue the explorers. Finally, on June 22, 1884, the rescuers came upon the wretched last encampment. Seven men out of the original twenty-five were still alive. One died on the return.

Staples-Herald Collection

176. The Greely survivors were brought to the Portsmouth Navy Yard to recuperate from their ordeal. The five men who had served under Greely were quartered in the Naval Hospital, while the Lieutenant and his family were given the use of the cottage seen in the background of this photograph. The survivors, from left to right, are Henry Biederbick, Maurice Connell, David L. Brainard, Adolphus W. Greely, Julius R. Frederick, and Francis Long. By the time that photographer L.V. Newell made this photograph in August, 1884, all six men had nearly regained their normal weight and appearance.

Staples-Herald Collection

177. The parade was more than a routine exercise at the turn of the century; it was a major medium of social expression and loomed large as a popular event in an otherwise rather quiet world. Here a large number of Portsmouth inhabitants gather at the intersection of State and Pleasant Streets to admire a series of floats evidently intended to celebrate the contributions of the manual trades. The vehicle in the foreground, prominently dedicated to the virtues of "Union Labor" was the entry of William J. Manson, a carpentry contractor who intended the latticework gazebo on the wagon to symbolize his livelihood.

Patch Collection

178. A parade moves in slightly disorganized array along State Street, a stately residential boulevard, in 1897. In the background is the 1891 Rockingham County Court House, then a new building but now, unfortunately, torn down, and replaced by a parking lot.

Patch Collection

179. On January 28, 1886, northern New England was hit by one of the heaviest ice storms on record. Shade trees lining every village and city street bent and broke under nature's pruning hook. The branches that remained, however, presented one of the most breathtaking spectacles ever seen. In Portsmouth, the energetic photographer L.V. Newell lost no time in getting his camera into the streets to record views that later sold widely as souvenirs. Here is Pleasant Street as a wagon and team (barely visible in the background) slowly proceed to gather fallen branches. At left is the Governor John Langdon Mansion; on the right is the tower of the 1807 Universalist Church and part of the facade of the Rev. Samuel Langdon House, both now lost to Portsmouth.

Patch Collection

178

179

180

181

180. One of the chief distinctions of the swift-flowing Piscataqua River, remarked upon even in the seventeenth century, is its freedom from ice in the lower reaches. Almost never is the river truly frozen, and only occasionally has it become severely choked with ice.

February 11, 1918, was probably the last time that ice solidly filled the lower river. This was not an instance of the river's actually freezing; rather, it appears that a mass of ice from Great Bay was precipitated downstream by a combination of weather conditions, and became firmly compacted when the current reversed itself with the changing tide.

The incident, which excited great curiosity among the people of Portsmouth, proved rather embarrassing to the passengers and crew of Navy Yard ferry 1048. As the little boat buffeted its way through the ice floes toward Kittery, the propeller suddenly "went bad" in midstream. The helpless boat drifted upriver on the incoming tide, and was soon surrounded by the ice massing in the upper harbor. The New Castle ferry, attempting to aid the larger boat, became firmly imbedded as well.

As soon as the ice had compacted sufficiently, a walkway of planks was laid to the stranded 1048, as recorded in this photograph. It appears that the last passengers were leaving when this picture was made, but at least two men can be discerned on the boat in the center of the picture, probably the New Castle ferry. At about 1:00 p.m. the tide changed and the stranded boats were freed once more.

Patch Collection

181. The point of land extending from Kittery toward New Castle had always created a swift, wily, and cross-grained current extremely hazardous to navigation. Named Henderson's Point in honor of its owners in the 1730s, this troublesome outcrop of rock earned a more colorful name from local rivermen, "Pull-and-Be-Damned Point." The turbulence off the point was a severe problem in the period before the introduction of steam tugboats, and even in the days of the "Great White Fleet," battleship captains are said to have been sufficiently intimidated by the current to prefer "to undergo the inconvenience of retaining the ships in the lower harbor, and receiving coal and other supplies by lighters, rather than incur the risks of passing through the channel at Henderson's Point."

182

183

Thus it was inevitable that the United States Government, which was sponsoring a modernization of the Portsmouth Navy Yard at the turn of the century, should want to remove the point. The contract for the work was awarded in August, 1902, on a bid of $749,000 by the Massachusetts Contracting Company. Specifications required the removal of 220,000 cubic yards of rock and 50,000 cubic feet of earth—an estimate which fell short of the work finally required to complete the job.

The final goal was to remove a 540-foot projection to a depth of thirty-five feet below mean low water, thereby creating a channel deep enough to float the largest ships of the time even at lowest tides. The first step in this project was the construction of a wooden cofferdam around the point's perimeter, inside which the engineers could excavate all but the rim of ledge by conventional means. This operation, nearly completed, is seen in this photograph.

Patch Collection

182. Inside the cofferdam, below the level of the river, workmen proceeded to dig and blast the ledge, using a railroad to carry away the debris. At the stage recorded in this photograph, they had succeeded in creating a well thirty-five feet deep within the outer perimeter of the ledge. The water which constantly leaked through the cofferdam and penetrated cracks in the stone was conducted by ditches to steam pumps, which discharged it back into the river.

It was finally decided, over the opposition of many authorities, that it would be possible to blast away the remaining outer shell of ledge in one mighty explosion—the largest ever planned by man. To effect this, it was necessary to drill scores of horizontal holes into the ledge to receive the dynamite. Some of these holes were as much as eighty-two feet deep, and required the fabrication of steel drills of unheard-of length. Thirty-five blacksmiths were rushed to the Navy Yard for this purpose. These men forged a series of drills for each hole, each drill being somewhat smaller in diameter, but three feet longer, than the drill that had preceded it in the hole. This technique required as many as twenty-seven separate drills for the deepest holes, starting with a short drill six inches in diameter and concluding with an eighty-five foot drill only an inch and three-quarters in diameter. The nine men in this photograph are shown carrying one of the drills of the latter dimensions.

Patch Collection

184

183. The mightiest explosion ever created by man shook the very bed of the Piscataqua River on July 22, 1905. This prodigious blast was created by the simultaneous discharge of fifty tons of dynamite which hurled water seventy-three feet into the air, and threw solid debris to a height of 170 feet.

Staples-Herald Collection

184. At the moment of the explosion, few observers had the temerity to approach the river. When the water and debris fell back into the stream a tidal wave ten feet high spread toward the New Castle shore, but quickly dissipated. Moments later, hundreds of observers trooped down to the river's edge in New Castle to savor the last moments of the greatest phenomenon most of them would ever witness. It was estimated that 35,000 people watched the explosion.

Patch Collection

185. Ten minutes after the explosion, the river was suddenly swarming with boats. The astounded observers found that most of the rim of rock had totally disappeared. The remaining outcroppings and the shattered debris on the river-bottom were not completely removed until 1911 or 1912. The project increased the width of the narrow channel by 350 feet, and removed the single feature that had prevented the Portsmouth Navy Yard from receiving a designation as a first-class naval station. (The jagged black line across this photo results from a crack in the glass negative.)

Patch Collection

185

Bibliography

Adams, Nathaniel. *Annals of Portsmouth . . . .* Portsmouth: Published by the Author, 1825.

Albee, John. *New Castle: Historic and Picturesque.* Boston: Cupples, Upham & Company, 1885.

Aldrich, Thomas Bailey. "An Old Town By the Sea," *Harper's New Monthly Magazine,* XLIX (October 1874), 632-650.

_____________. *An Old Town By the Sea.* Boston: Houghton, Mifflin and Company, 1894.

Attractive Bits Along Shore: Rye Beach, Portsmouth, Isles of Shoals, Old York, Kittery Point. Portland, Maine: H. Wilbur Hayes, n.d.

Banks, Charles Edward. *History of York, Maine.* 3 vols. Baltimore: Regional Publishing Company, 1967.

Barnard, Henry. *School Architecture.* New York: A.S. Barnes & Co., 1849.

Benjamin, Asher. *The American Builder's Companion.* Reprint of the 6th (1827) edition. New York: Dover Publications, 1969.

Bishop, J. Leander. *A History of American Manufacturers From 1608 to 1860 . . . .* 2 vols. Philadelphia: Edward Young & Co., 1861.

Boyd, David F., comp. *Extracts From the Daily Log Book, U.S. Navy Yard, Portsmouth, New Hampshire, October 15, 1819-December 17, 1929.*

Brewster, Charles W. *Rambles About Portsmouth.* 2 vols. Portsmouth: C.W. Brewster & Son, 1859-1869.

Brighton, Raymond. *The Portsmouth Savings Bank, 1823-1958: An Adventure in Community Service.*

Chapelle, Howard I. *The History of the American Sailing Navy: The Ships and Their Development.* New York: Bonanza Books, 1949.

Charlton, Edwin A. *New Hampshire As It Is.* Claremont, N.H.: Tracy and Sanford, 1855.

Chase, Robert S. and James L. Garvin. "Portsmouth: An Architectural Evolution, 1664-1890," *New Hampshire Profiles,* XIX, xii (December 1970), 23-54.

Colby, H.B. "A Glass of Ale," *The Granite Monthly,* XXXVII, i (July 1904), 3-13.

Contract for the Construction of a Dwelling House for Capt. John Hill, 1698. Owned by the Society for the Preservation of New England Antiquities, Boston, Massachusetts.

Craig, Lawrence R. *Three Centuries of Religious Living.* Portsmouth, 1966.

Cummings, O.R. *Trolleys to York Beach: The Portsmouth Dover & York Street Railway.* n.p.

Curtis, Chester B., comp. *Bi-Centennial Souvenir, New Castle, New Hampshire, 1693-1893.*

Darrah, William Culp. *Stereo Views: A History of Stereographs in America and Their Collection.* Gettysburg, Pennsylvania: Times and News Publishing Co., 1964.

Davis, Franklin Ware. *Old St. John's Parish, Portsmouth.* (Reprinted from *New England Magazine,* November 1894).

DeNormandie, Rev. James, et. al. *Langdon Park, Portsmouth, N.H. . . . . An Account of Building the Park, and the Opening Exercises, May 25, 1876.* Portsmouth: Charles W. Gardner, 1876.

Downey, Joseph T. *The Cruise of the Portsmouth, 1845-1847: A Sailor's View of the Naval Conquest of California.* ed. Howard Lamar. New Haven: Yale University Press, 1958.

Falconer, William. *Falconer's Marine Dictionary.* Improved and Enlarged by Dr. William Burney. London: Printed for T. Cadell and W. Davies and J. Murray, 1815.

Fetherstonhaugh, R.C. *Charles Fleetford Sise, 1834-1918.* Montreal: Gazette Printed Company, 1944.

Fitts, Rev. James Hill. *History of Newfields, N.H.* Concord, N.H., 1912.

Folsom, Elizabeth Knowles. *Genealogy of the Folsom Family, 1638-1938.* 2 vols. Rutland, Vt.: Tuttle Publishing Co., 1938.

Foss, Gerald D. "Franklin Block," *The Trestle Board,* October 1964.

Foss, Gerald D. and Woodbury S. Adams. *Three Centuries of Freemasonry in New Hampshire.*, ed. Enzo Serafini. Grand Lodge of New Hampshire, Concord, N.H., 1972.

Foster, Sarah H. *The Portsmouth Guide Book . . . .* Portsmouth: Portsmouth Journal Job Print, 1896.

Frank Jones Brewery Advertisement, containing description and map of plant, n.d.

Garvin, James L. *Bradbury Johnson, Builder-Architect.* Unpublished M.A. Thesis, University of Delaware, June 1969.

_____________. "Portsmouth and the Piscataqua: Social History and Material Culture," *Historical New Hampshire,* XXVI, ii (Summer 1971), 3-48.

Gilman, Isabel Ambler. "Women's Clubs," a poem, *The Granite Monthly,* XXXIII, i (July 1902), 52-53.

Gurney, Caleb S. *Portsmouth, Historic and Picturesque . . . .* Portsmouth, 1902.

Hackett, Frank W. *Memoir of William H.Y. Hackett . . . .* Portsmouth, 1879.

Hartford, F.W. "Building Ships at Portsmouth," *The Granite Monthly,* XV, iv (April 1919), 166-171.

Hazlett, Charles A. *History of Rockingham County, New Hampshire and Representative Citizens.* Chicago: Richmond-Arnold Publishing Company, 1915.

Historic American Buildings Survey, Library of Congress. "Boyd-Raynes House," NH-5, 25 sheets, measured drawings.

History of the Portsmouth Naval Shipyard, 1800-1958.

Holland, Francis Ross, Jr. *America's Lighthouses.* Brattleboro, Vermont: The Stephen Greene Press, 1972.

Hollis, Ira N. *The Frigate Constitution: The Central Figure of the Navy Under Sail.* Boston: Houghton, Mifflin and Company, 1900.

Howells, John Mead. *The Architectural Heritage of the Piscataqua: Houses and Gardens of the Portsmouth District of Maine and New Hampshire.* New York: Architectural Book Publishing Company, 1965.

_______________. *Lost Examples of Colonial Architecture: Buildings that Have Disappeared or Been So Altered as to be Denatured.* New York: Dover Publications, 1963.

Hurd, D. Hamilton, comp. *History of Rockingham and Strafford Counties, New Hampshire, With Biographical Sketches of Many of Its Pioneers and Prominent Men.* Philadelphia: J.W. Lewis & Co., 1882.

Ingersoll, Daniel Winthrop, Jr. *Settlement Archaeology at Puddle Dock.* 2 vols. Unpublished Ph.D. Dissertation, Harvard University, 1971.

Insurance Maps of Portsmouth, Rockingham County, New Hampshire, Sept. 1910. New York: Sanborn Map Company, 1910.

"The Isles of Shoals," *Harper's New Monthly Magazine,* XLIX (October 1874), 663-676.

Jenness, John Scribner. *The Isles of Shoals: An Historical Sketch.* New York: Hurd and Houghton, 1875.

Laighton, Cedric. *Letters to Celia Written During the Years 1860-1875 to Celia Laighton Thaxter by her Brother Cedric Laighton,* ed. Frederick T. McGill, Jr. Boston: The Star Island Corporation, 1972.

Laighton, Oscar. *Ninety Years At the Isles of Shaols.* Andover: Massachusetts, 1929.

Lewis, Emanuel Raymond. *Seacoast Fortifications of the United States: An Introductory History.* Washington: Smithsonian Institution Press, 1970.

Maddock, S. Booth. "Strawbery Banke, Circa 1915," *New Hampshire Profiles,* XVII, ix (September 1968), 48-49.

Margeson, Henry B., comp. *Biographical Roster: Members of the Mechanic Fire Society.* Portsmouth: Mechanic Fire Society, 1966.

Mathes, Frances A. and Charles A. Hazlett, ed. *An Historical Calendar of Portsmouth.* Portsmouth: The Randall Press, 1907.

Moran, Geoffrey P. "The Post Office and Custom House at Portsmouth, New Hampshire, and Its Architect, Ammi Burnham Young," *Old-Time New England,* LVII, iv (Spring 1967), 85-102.

Morgan, Charles S. *New England Coasting Schooners.* Salem: Massachusetts: The American Neptune, 1963.

Navy Department. *Dictionary of American Naval Fighting Ships.* Vol. I-. Washington, 1959-present.

The New Hampshire Gazette, files in Portsmouth Athenaeum and in the Strawbery Banke Library.

Nutter, James. "The Experience of James Nutter." Unpublished manuscript. Copy in possession of James L. Garvin.

Parker, W.J. Lewis. *The Great Coal Schooners of New England, 1870-1909.* Mystic, Connecticut: The Marine Historical Association, 1948.

Parsons, Langdon B. *History of the Town of Rye, New Hampshire . . .* Concord, N.H.: Rumford Printing Company, 1905.

Patterson, Adoniram J. *Eulogy on Abraham Lincoln, Delivered in Portsmouth, N.H., April 19, 1865. And an Account of The Obsequies Observed by the City.* Portsmouth: C.W. Brewster & Son, 1865.

The Portsmouth Book. Boston: George H. Ellis, n.d.

Portsmouth Daily Chronicle, files in the Strawbery Banke Library.

The Portsmouth Daily Herald, files in the Strawbery Banke Library.

The Portsmouth Journal, files in the Portsmouth Athenaeum.

Portsmouth Directories, 1821 to present, files in the Portsmouth Athenaeum.

Portsmouth in the Year 1824. Portsmouth: First National Bank, 1912.

Portsmouth, Town of. *Receipts and Expenditures of the Town of Portsmouth By the Overseers of the Poor, School Committee, and Selectmen For the Year Ending March 24, 1834.* Portsmouth, 1834.

Portsmouth, Town of. Vital Records, City Hall, Portsmouth, N.H.

Potter, E.B. *The Naval Academy History of the United States Navy.* New York: Thomas Y. Crowell Company, 1971.

Powell, Theodore. *The Long Rescue.* Garden City, N.Y.: Doubleday & Company, 1960.

[Randall, Peter]. Article on Freezing of Piscataqua River, *New Hampshire Profiles,* XXI, i (January 1972), 16.

The Re-union of '73: The Second Reception of the Sons and Daughters of Portsmouth, Resident Abroad, July 4, 1873. Portsmouth: Charles W. Gardner, n.d.

Rockingham County Records, Rockingham County Administration Building, Exeter, New Hampshire.

Rowe, William Hutchinson. *The Maritime History of Maine: Three Centuries of Shipbuilding & Seafaring.* Maine: The Bond Wheelwright Company, n.d.

Rutledge, Lyman V. *The Isles of Shoals in Lore and Legend.* Barre, Massachusetts: Barre Publishers, 1965.

Shipton, Clifford K. "Samuel Langdon," *Sibley's Harvard Graduates,* X (1736-1740). Boston: Massachusetts Historical Society, 1958.

Spinney, Frank O. "B.C. Gilman, An Ingenious Yankee Craftsman," *Antiques,* XLIV (September 1943), 116-119.

Stackpole, Everett S. *Old Kittery and Her Families.* Lewiston, Maine: Press of Lewiston Journal Company, 1903.

Stickney, Joseph L. *Admiral Dewey at Manila and the Complete Story of the Philippines . . . .* Philadelphia: Elliott Publishing Company, 1899.

Sullivan, Timothy P. "The Portsmouth Navy Yard, The New Dry Dock, and Henderson's Point," *The Granite Monthly,* XXXVI, ii (February 1904), 65-68.

Taft, Robert. *Photography and the American Scene: A Social History, 1839-1889.* New York: The Macmillan Company, 1938.

Thaxter, Celia. *Among the Isles of Shoals.* Sanbornville, New Hampshire: Wake-Brook House, n.d. (Original ed. 1873).

Thaxter, Celia. *The Heavenly Guest With Other Unpublished Writings,* ed. Oscar Laighton. Andover, Massachusetts: Smith and Coutts Co., 1935.

______________. *Letters of Celia Thaxter,* ed. A.F. and R.L. Boston: Houghton, Mifflin and Company, 1895.

Thaxter, Rosamond. *Sandpiper: The Life and Letters of Celia Thaxter and Her Home on The Isles of Shoals* . . . . Francestown, New Hampshire: Marshall Jones Company, 1963.

Thomas, Isaiah. *The History of Printing in America.* 2 vols. Worcester, Massachusetts: Isaiah Thomas, Jun., 1810.

Todd, A.L. *Abandoned: The Story of the Greely Arctic Expedition, 1881-1884.* New York: McGraw-Hill Book Company, 1961.

Town and City Atlas of the State of New Hampshire . . . . Boston: D.H. Hurd & Co., 1892.

Varrell, William M. *Rye on the Rocks: The Tale of a Town.* Portsmouth, 1962.

______________. *Summer by-the-Sea: The Golden Era of Victorian Beach Resorts.* Portsmouth, 1972.

Winslow, Richard Elliott. "He Built an Empire With Ale," *New Hampshire Profiles,* XVIII, vi (June 1969), 36-39 and XVIII, vii (July 1969), 29-31, 45-47.

Young, James Rankin and J. Hampton Moore. *History of Our War with Spain* . . . . n.p., 1898.